from FORGIVEN to forgiving

Jay Adams

CALVARY PRESS
Box 805 Amityville, NY 11701

First printing of soft cover edition- February 1994

CALVARY PRESS
Box 805, Amityville, NY 11701
1-800-789-8175

ISBN: 1 - 879737 - 12- 4

2 4 6 8 10 9 7 5 3 1

Cover and book design by Michael Rotolo

Publisher's Special thanks to:
Pastor Dave Dykstra and Jean Horjus of Monroe Bible
Chapel in Franklin, New Jersey who greatly encouraged
us to republish this very helpful book, and to the author
Dr. Jay E. Adams for his gracious permission to do so.

Unless otherwise noted, Scripture quotations are from *The Christian Counselor's New Testament* by Jay E. Adams,© 1977 by Presbyterian and Reformed Publishing Company. Other quotations are from *The Modern Language Bible: The Berkeley Version in Modern English* (MLB), © 1945, 1959, 1969 by Zondervan Publishing House, used by permission; and the *Holy Bible, New International Version* (NIV), © 1973, 1978, 1984, International Bible Society. Used by permission of Zondervan Bible Publishers.

Recommended Dewey Decimal Classification: 248.4

PRINTED IN THE UNITED STATES OF AMERICA

Contents

to
BRANDON JAY
with joy and hope

Foreword

At a time when the church is rediscovering the importance of forgiveness and restoration, *From Forgiven to Forgiving,* is a practical approach to reconciling relationships and entering into a deeper walk with the Lord.

Before we can enter into any lasting relationship with another, we must learn how to forgive since we all hurt one another. The Bible says, "forgiving one another. . . ." It does not simply say, "forgiving others," but "forgiving one another." It is a mutual cooperative venture. Not only do we need to forgive, we also need to receive forgiveness. It is the indispensable sign of a Christian.

Each of us stands daily in need of the forgiveness of God; therefore, we need to hear what God has to say to us about that. Jesus taught us to pray, "Forgive us our debts, as we also forgive our debtors." It is clear then that unless we forgive, we are not forgiven.

This is an aspect that seems to have been forgotten in our churches today. And, as forgiveness is usually a painful process, it is one that is quite often ignored.

From Forgiven to Forgiving, takes the reader through every aspect of this critical issue, from the biblical definition of forgiveness, to a step-by-step guide to putting these truths into practice. Jay Adams has given some clear insights and helpful suggestions on how to become a forgiving person.

If you have ever struggled with the concept of forgiveness, I encourage you to read this book. May the Holy Spirit reveal to you once again the reality that your sins are forgiven by the atoning blood of Jesus. And may you in turn forgive others.

Dr. D. James Kennedy
Pastor
Coral Ridge Presbyterian Church
Fort Lauderdale, Florida

Preface

I have written this book for two purposes:

    1. To provide a simple, easy-to-read reference volume for the average Christian—something he can read, then turn to again and again as the need arises. It is my hope that the volume will find wide acceptance for this purpose among God's people and will be one means of bringing the church to an acknowledgment of the importance of forgiveness.

    2. I have tried to encounter most of the principal errors currently believed or taught by various persons in the Christian church. It is not my desire to attack people who hold differing views from mine, that I consider unbiblical, but to warn you about those views and point out why they are unacceptable.

    I considered providing examples and case studies of each point throughout the text. But I was concerned that to do so would make it too cumbersome and thus decrease

the value of the book as a quick reference volume. Therefore, I have kept such material to the minimum.

It is my prayer that the volume I now send forth will find its way into many hands and do much good in the church of Christ. I hope that husbands and wives, children and parents, businessmen and employees, and officers and members of the church will all receive help.

This is the sort of book that may be handed to persons receiving counseling to supplement the counseling itself. It could be used as a week-day prayer meeting guide to stimulate discussion and Bible study. It might be used in a Sunday School class or a youth group. I have attempted to produce a book that will be readily understandable to persons of most ages and have endeavored to make it as widely adaptable as possible.

If you find the book helpful, pass it on to others or suggest to the officers of your church that they may be able to use it in one or more of the ways mentioned in the previous paragraph. But whatever else you do, remember: forgiveness is an important condition to fellowship with the Heavenly Father. It is not an option. God commands it. Nor may we guess about how to forgive, whom to forgive, when to forgive, or how often to forgive. God has not left us without explicit information. The biblical data are not difficult to understand in spite of the fact that many seem to have found ways in which to misunderstand them. Mostly these erroneous ideas come from two sources: (1) psychology, which some attempt to integrate with biblical truth, thereby distorting the truth in favor of the psychology; (2) failure to study carefully the biblical teachings, substituting guesses and surmises instead.

May our great God, who in His Son brought forgiveness to us, bless you as you seek to apply these truths to your life.

Introduction

You are sitting in the front row before a huge screen, waiting for the show to begin. It is no ordinary show. The auditorium is crowded; every seat is taken. People have dragged chairs into the aisles. Some people are standing around the edges of the room; others are looking through the windows from outside.

Why all the interest in this particular show? There is a good reason. The movie that is about to begin is the unexpurgated, premier showing of *your life story!*

"The unexpurgated version?" you ask.

Yes, the whole thing! *Nothing* has been deleted. There, in vivid Technicolor, you will see everything you have ever done—all those things you did when you thought no one was looking, the things you've long since gladly forgotten. Moreover, on the sound track you will hear all you ever

said—even those things you muttered under your breath ("If I could get my hands on that dried-up old prune, I'd wring her neck!"). Nothing will be omitted.

Suppose that this film is able to out-Hollywood Hollywood. On that screen, in sound and color, will be projected everything you have ever *thought*. All the things you allowed yourself to wallow in—the things you would like to have done if you thought you could have gotten away with them. Why, that would be the juiciest part of all.

Tell me, if all your friends, relatives, and enemies have gathered in such profusion to see that film, would you be there at the end of the show to take a bow? If it were my life story, you wouldn't find me there five minutes into the show! And, if you are honest, I think you will admit you wouldn't be there either.

"I'm glad no one has the film of my life," you say.

Ah, but Someone does! *God* has the film. What's more, He's planning to show it (Luke 12:2-3)—not before such a paltry crowd as this but before the entire universe! And there won't be anywhere to hide.

There is only one way you can avoid that terrible event: get God to destroy the film. That, of course, is why Jesus came. He came to die for the sins of His people. All who are ashamed of their lives, who recognize that they have sinned before God, and who come to the risen Saviour in faith saying, "Jesus, I believe You died for my sins, taking the punishment that I deserve" will be forgiven. God will take the film and throw it into the depths of the deepest sea. He will remove it as far as the East is from the West. He will remember their sins against them no more.

Forgiveness—what a wonderful thing it is! Forgiveness is man's greatest need. Without it he is doomed to spend eternity in hell suffering for his sins. With it, he will spend eternity in heaven with God enjoying the eternal fruits of Christ's righteousness.

WHAT ABOUT UNBELIEVERS?

If you have never been forgiven by God and recognize that you dare not come into His presence unforgiven, laden with the guilt of your sins, then trust Christ as Saviour today. He will cleanse your record before God and give you a new life here below, empowered by the Spirit and directed by God's Word, so that you may begin to serve Christ here and now as your Lord.

But this book is not about unforgiven people being forgiven; it is about forgiven persons—God's children—becoming *forgiving* persons. It is about the problem of believers forgiving one another.

The Apostle Paul wrote, "Be kind, tenderhearted, forgiving one another just as God, for Christ's sake, has forgiven you" (Eph. 4:32). God expects His children, who have been forgiven a huge debt, to forgive others who by comparison owe so little (see Matt. 18:21-35).

Forgiveness is the oil that keeps the machinery of the Christian home and church running smoothly. In a world where even those who have been declared perfect in Christ sin, there is much to forgive. Christians who must work together closely find themselves denting each others' fenders, now and then taking out a taillight or two, and at times even having head-on collisions. Under such conditions, forgiveness is what keeps things from breaking down completely.

"But all too many Christian homes and churches are breaking down," you object.

Exactly. That's why this book was written. It seems as though many Christians have forgotten all about forgiveness. Instead, they go about demanding that others treat them as they think they should, and when that doesn't happen, they whine about how they have lost self-esteem. Indeed some seem to have learned so little about forgiveness that there is little to forget. Still others may have bought into all sorts of wrong ideas about forgiveness.

[7]

This book is my attempt to alleviate the problem by providing you with a working knowledge of what the Bible says about forgiveness. It is my prayer that God will use it to help you, and the members of your home and church, to function in ways that better please Him.

1 WHAT IS FORGIVENESS?

A s you will discover later in this book the correct answer to the question at the head of this chapter is essential. In any study, a proper understanding of basic issues is important early on as a foundation on which to build structures of truth. That is certainly the case when considering forgiveness. Until this basic question has been satisfactorily addressed, you will address other questions regarding forgiveness either unsatisfactorily or not at all.

"I'm not so sure I see your point. Doesn't everyone know what forgiveness is? Why, when someone has wronged me, I expect him to come and apologize. Then I tell him, 'That's OK.' That's forgiveness isn't it?"

No, I'm afraid it isn't. You see, many wrong ideas go about masquerading as forgiveness that are not biblical forgiveness at all. Indeed, probably most Christians have wrong ideas about forgiveness, just like those in the previous paragraph.

"Well, I can't see where there's anything wrong with the ideas I just expressed. I'm baffled, I always thought forgiveness was one of those areas, unlike baptism and predestination, where there is no argument. You're going to have to do some pretty fancy talking to convince me that I don't understand what forgiveness is."

I realize that. I also recognize that discussion of forgiveness is commonly neglected because everyone thinks he understands it when actually he doesn't. Take, for instance, your notion of "apologizing." Where do you find that in the Bible? Do biblical writers, like many Christians writing today, ever equate "apologizing" with seeking forgiveness?

"Well. . . no. I guess not. But everyone knows that apologizing is what you do when you seek forgiveness."

Frankly, I'm afraid that's what most Christians do think. But, as you will discover later on, apologizing is not only unscriptural, it is the world's unsatisfactory substitute for forgiveness. I don't want to discuss apologizing now, but I bring it up because you mentioned it. And what you said is a good example of what I have been talking about—wrong assumptions that are so widespread that few ever think to question them.

"Well, I guess I can't think of anything in the Bible that tells us to apologize, so perhaps there is a thing or two that I can learn about forgiveness after all. But I still can't see where apologizing is a substitute for forgiveness."

We'll come to that in good time, but first, as I said, it is important to build a proper biblical foundation for all such discussions. That's why, at this point, I want to talk about forgiveness itself. What is forgiveness anyway? There are at least two ways to answer that question.

What Forgiveness Does and Is

We can talk about what forgiveness *does* (i.e., what it accomplishes). To do so is to speak practically, in terms of its results. In such an answer our response would begin with words like these: "Forgiveness is a process whereby...."

That's one way to answer the question. Perhaps it is the principal way in which it has been answered by theologians and preachers over the years. As important as that answer is—and we shall say more about it at another place in this book—it is not what I want to consider here.

The other way in which the question "What is forgiveness?" may be answered is to discuss its nature or essence. That is to say, having boiled all else away, what is the irreducible element that is left that makes forgiveness forgiveness?

For many years I read about forgiveness, talked about forgiveness, preached forgiveness. And most of what I said was true. However, there was something missing, something that remained vague, unexplained—something intangible that dogged my steps. Then on day I began to think deeply about forgiveness. In the process I asked myself, "What is forgiveness anyway?" You know, I didn't have an answer. I simply couldn't state what, in its essence, forgiveness is. "Is it a feeling?" I wondered. But that didn't seem right. "Doesn't God require me to forgive my brother, whether I feel like it or not?"[1] Unlike modern discussions of forgiveness, there is nothing in the Bible about "feelings of forgiveness" or "having forgiving feelings" toward another. No, that is clearly the wrong path to an answer. Well, then, what is forgiveness?

Thinking about the matter, I remembered that Paul tells us in Ephesians 4:32 to "forgive one another just as God, for Christ's sake, has forgiven" us. "Among other things," I reasoned, "that means our forgiveness is to be modeled after God's. In order to find out what forgiveness is I must study God's forgiveness." At last I have found the key to unlock the door to the meaning of forgiveness.

Obviously, when God forgives, He does not simply sit in the heavens and emote. So forgiveness isn't a feeling. If it were, we would never know that we have been forgiven. No, when God forgives, He goes on record. He *says* so. He declares, "I will not remember your sins" (Isa 43:25; see also Jer. 31:34). Isn't that wonderful? When He forgives, God *lets us know* that He will no longer hold our sins against us. If forgiveness were merely an emotional experience, we would not know that we were forgiven. But praise God, we do, because forgiveness is a process at the

end of which God declares that the matter of sin has been dealt with once and for all.

Now, what is that declaration? What does God do when He goes on record saying that our sins are forgiven? God makes a promise. Forgiveness is not a feeling; forgiveness is a *promise*!

Forgiveness Is a Promise

Never forget that fact. It is one of the most stupendous facts of all time. When our God forgives us, He promises that He will not remember our sins against us anymore. That is wonderful!

"Yes, I recognize that is what Isaiah and Jeremiah say. But I've always had a problem with such statements. How can God, who knows all things—past, present, and future— ever forget anything? How can He forget our sins?"

He doesn't.

"But doesn't it say that He won't remember *our sins?"*

Yes, it does, but that's not the same thing as *forgetting* them. Obviously, the omniscient God who created and sustains the universe does not forget, but He can "not remember." You see, forgetting is passive and is something that we human beings, not being omniscient, do. "Not remembering" is active; it is a promise whereby one person (in this case, God) determines not to remember the sins of another *against him*.[2] To "not remember" is simply a graphic way of saying, "I will not bring up these matters to you or others in the future. I will bury them and not exhume the bones to beat you over the head with them. I will never use these sins against you."

"So now I see the difference! You have answered a perplexing problem that I have never been able to resolve before. I am certainly glad to have a clear, satisfying explanation of that matter at last. Perhaps there is more to forgiveness than at first meets the eye. Probably I have a lot more to learn than I realized."

Yes, and there are important implications of the facts that we have discussed in this chapter having to do with mutual forgiveness among the brethren that I must discuss in a later chapter. For now, perhaps you can see the importance of beginning with the basics.

2 WHAT DOES THIS MEAN TO YOU?

ಬಬಬಬಬಬಬಬಬಬಬಬಬಬಬಬಬಬಬಬ

Perhaps the easiest way to begin to discuss the implications of the previous chapter is to plunge right ahead into a principal passage on forgiveness in which Jesus had the following words to say:

"Be on your guard. If your brother sins, rebuke him; if he repents, forgive him. And if he sins against you seven times a day and returns to you seven times saying, 'I repent,' forgive him."

Then the apostles said to the Lord, "Increase our faith!"

But the Lord said, "If you have faith like a mustard seed, you could say to this mulberry tree, 'Be uprooted and be planted in the sea,' and it would obey you. Which of you, if he had a slave plowing or tending sheep, would say to him when he comes in from the field, 'Come and recline at the table right away'? Wouldn't he say to him, 'Prepare something for me to eat, and when you are dressed, serve me until I have finished eating and drinking, and then you can eat and drink'? Does he thank the slave because he did what he was commanded? So you too, when you do everything that you are commanded, say, 'We are unprofitable slaves; we have simply done what we ought to have done.'" (Luke 17:3-10)

A Warning

The words, "Be on your guard" (v. 3) may seem an unusual introduction to a discussion of forgiveness, yet that is how Jesus began. He must have had a reason. Think about it for a minute.

Renowned preacher Charles Spurgeon, who had a very serious case of gout, was once approached by a man who claimed that his rheumatism was more painful than Spurgeon's gout. Now, you simply didn't say things like that to Spurgeon and get away with it! Spurgeon replied: "I'll tell you the difference between rheumatism and gout: Put your finger into a vise and turn it until you can't stand the pain; that's rheumatism. Now, give it three more turns; that's gout!"

Jesus warns you because in verse 3, there is both rheumatism and gout. In verses 3-10 there is some of the most difficult teaching in the New Testament. It is not difficult to understand, just difficult to put into practice. Jesus warns you that what He is about to say will be hard to swallow. So Christian, get ready for it: "Be on your guard."

The Rheumatism

"If your brother sins, rebuke him; if he repents, forgive him." Those are difficult words. The first is hard, extremely hard, and the second even more so. But, let's look first at the rheumatism: "If your brother sins, rebuke him."

As verse 4 makes clear, the sin about which Jesus is speaking is a sin against *you*. The question arises immediately: How do you handle sins against you? Think about that a bit. How *do* you?

Here you are, minding your own business, provoking no one to anger, just surveying the scene. All of a sudden, literally or figuratively (probably the latter) your brother (or sister) comes along, stomps all over your toes, and disappears over the hill. There you stand—through no fault

of your own—with ten toes flattened out like ten silver dollar pancakes. They hurt! Now, what do you do next?

Well, some begin to whine and feel sorry for themselves. They look for the syrup and pour it all over their feet. They hold a pity party and invite others to join in. But that isn't what Jesus said to do.

Others get furious. They storm about making their wrath known, and either go after the brother to tell him off or charge around their home kicking chairs or children instead. Neither is that which Jesus said to do.

A third group, more pious than the rest, go around the congregation displaying their flattened toes to as many as will view them, saying, "Now, you understand that I don't mean to gossip in telling you what so-and-so did. I'm just warning you so that you can protect yourself from such injury in the future." But Jesus didn't tell you to do that either.

What did He say?

Jesus says, "Rebuke him." That's rheumatism!

What He tells you to do is go after the brother, take him (gently) by the collar, and say, "Brother, look at my toes!"

Notice, Jesus doesn't allow you to go tell others about it, to sit in the corner and feel sorry for yourself, to take it out on others in your vicinity, or even to tell the elders. He says go to the one who tread on your toes, and talk to him about it.

Why You Should Go

"But why should I go?" you ask. "I didn't start anything. I was an innocent bystander, just surveying the scene when he (or she) came along and flattened my toes. Shouldn't he come to me?"

That is a reasonable question and one that many persons ask. The trouble is that most of them answer it the wrong way. Jesus is saying, in effect, that whenever your brother or sister wrongs you, that obligates you to take action. No matter how innocent you may have been, you are obligated to go to him.

"But isn't he obligated to come to me? I don't see why his sin against me obligates me to act; let him come to me."

Yes, as a matter of fact, if he has sinned against you, he is obligated to come to you. But that is another passage, to which we are not currently referring (Matt. 5:23-24). The command in Luke is for you to go to him. Both commands are important; you should go and he should go. Ideally, you ought to meet each other on the way.

"Well, if he's obligated to go, I don't see why I must do so too."

Let me try to explain. You haven't seen your friend Jane for several months; she's been away traveling. This morning you see her at church, seated on the opposite side of the building. You can't wait till the service is over to talk to her. At the conclusion of the service, you rush around the pews and happily call to her, "Jane! Jane! It's so good to see you!" But Jane sticks her nose into the air, turns on her heel, and sails out of the church as rapidly as possible, without so much as a "how do you do?"

You stand there hurt and perplexed. If you respond as many do, you'll say, "Hurrruuummmph! If that's the way she's going to act, then so be it! I can wait till she comes down off her high horse and wants to talk. Then maybe I'll be ready to do so and maybe I won't!"

But, you see, Jesus won't let you do that. He tells you to go after her and show her your toes. Suppose you do. Having recovered from the shock, you say to yourself, "Something's wrong here. I've got to get to the bottom of it. I can't have this happen to Jane and me." So you hightail it out of the church after her. There she is over at her car. You go over and you say, "Jane! What's wrong? I was so glad to see you home again that I rushed over to see you after church, but when I called to you, you stuck your nose in the air and left. What's wrong?"

Perhaps Jane's response will be something like this: "Oh no! Mary, I didn't even hear or see you! You see, I caught a bad cold on my trip abroad, and the pastor preached forever today, and I left my tissues in the car, and I thought for sure I was going to drip all over my new dress and my Bible. That's why I put my nose back and rushed out here to get those tissues. I was so preoccupied with all that I didn't see or hear you."

"Stupid illustration," you say.

Yes, but I chose it because I have known case after case where friendships have been destroyed over misunderstandings just as stupid as that. Don't you see? You are obligated to go because the brother or sister may not know that he (she) stepped on your toes. It may all be a misunderstanding. So, the rule is:

The one with the sore toes goes because he's the one who always knows.

Rebuking—What It Means Here

It is important here to distinguish between things that differ. There are two words in the New Testament for rebuking. One means "to so prosecute a case against another that he is convicted of the crime of which he was accused." Needless to say, that is not the word used here.

The other, which Jesus uses in this connection, means "to rebuke tentatively." That is to say, when you go, you must do so with caution. You go with the facts as you see them. You present the facts. Then you wait for any possible forthcoming explanation that might clear up a misunderstanding or that might mitigate the situation. If there is none, the offense has been committed, and if your brother or sister repents, you are to forgive him or her. If he refuses, that may possibly lead to informal (and eventually formal) church discipline. But we are getting ahead of ourselves. Right now, it is important to stress that when you go, you give the brother or sister an opportunity to explain any misunderstanding, if he or she can.

So much for the rheumatism; now for the gout: "If he repents, forgive him."

"That's the gout? I thought you said that the second half of verse 3 was more difficult than the first. I certainly don't see how rebuking him is easier than forgiving him if he repents."

Well, there is a good reason for Jesus' warning. If you let your guard down, you could easily be lulled into thinking so. But let me sketch a brief scenario for you.

There you are once again, simply standing there surveying the scene, doing no one any harm, provoking no one to wrath or anger, when all of a sudden, out of a clear blue sky, *"pow!"* Literally or figuratively (probably the latter), your brother hits you right on the old beezer! There you are, nourishing and cherishing your sore nose when here he comes, hat in hand, shuffling up.

He says, "You know what I did?"

You reply, "I certainly do; why'dja do it?"

"Well," he says, "you see, I've got this terrible temper, and I got upset, and you were the closest one around, so I. . . . Oh, I'm sorry. It was nothing personal. Will you forgive me?"

"Yeah," you say, molding your nose back into shape, *"but don't do it again."*

Five minutes later, just when your nose is beginning to feel a little bit better, "pow!" He does it again! And again he comes, hat in hand, shuffling toward you. "Do you know what I did?"

"I sure do. Why'dja do it? I thought you said you weren't going to do that again!"

"Well, you see, I've got this temper, and—"

"I know about your temper."

"Well, you can't do much to overcome a temper like this in five minutes! Will you forgive me?"

"Yes, *But don't do it again!"*

Not once, not twice, but seven times in the same day (literally or figuratively) he socks you on the old beezer. And seven times, he returns asking for forgiveness. What will you do?

Well, there are many who will say, "Once, yes; twice, maybe, three times—no way."

But Jesus said, "And if he sins against you seven times a day and returns to you seven times saying, 'I repent,' forgive him" (v. 4). That's gout; it hurts!

Now, of course, by "seven times" Jesus didn't mean *only* seven times; he just rounded it off with that number, meaning, in effect, "as often as it happens that way, you must forgive him."

The apostles understood well enough that this was "gout": "Then the apostles said to the Lord, 'Whew! Increase our faith'" (v. 5). Of course, there was no "whew!" because the Greeks didn't have a word for it. But that certainly expresses their attitude. They were saying, "If we have to do that, Lord, we're going to need more faith!"

That was a pretty good response on their part, wasn't it?

No! It wasn't. It was a pious cop-out! Look how Jesus handled it: "But the Lord said, 'If you have faith like a mustard seed, you could say to this mulberry tree "Be uprooted and be planted in the sea," and it would obey you'" (v. 6). What was He saying? He was saying, "I told you to do something and here you are making excuses why you can't. You say, 'When I get more faith, I'll obey. But not before.' I tell you it isn't a matter of how much faith you have. If you have any faith at all, even a smidgen the size of a mustard seed, you could do wonders with it. Don't tell Me you need more faith. This is a matter of obedience, not a matter of the amount of faith you have."

So, the excuse "when I get more faith" is shattered.

But notice also how Jesus structured His example: "If he sins...seven times *a day*...and returns seven times *saying* 'I repent.'" that wording eliminates a second common excuse for not obeying.

People will, say, "But if he hits me in the nose (literally or figuratively) seven times a day, his repentance can't be sincere; after all, 'by their fruit shall you know them.' I would forgive him if I saw any fruit appropriate to repentance."

But when did you ever see a watermelon grow in *a day*? A cantaloupe? Even a grape? Jesus structures His example in such a way that no such excuse could be forthcoming. Fruit takes time to grow. It takes cultivation, work, etc. And, as Jesus set it up, the man comes *"saying"* he is repentant. In love, "believing all things, hoping all things," you must take his naked word for it. No, you may not say, "When I see the fruit, I'll forgive." The second excuse has evaporated.

But before the third is brought to bear, Jesus tells a story:

> Which of you, if he had a slave plowing or tending sheep, would say to him when he comes in from the field, 'Come and recline at the table right away'? Wouldn't he say to him, 'Prepare something for me to eat, and when you are dressed, serve me until I have finished eating and drinking, and then you can eat and drink'? Does he thank the slave because he did what he was commanded? So you too, when you do everything you are commanded, say, 'We are unprofitable slaves; we have simply done what we ought to have done.'" (Luke 17:7-10)

Picture this slave, who has been working under a hot Palestinian sun all day long, coming home. He's tired,

thirsty, hungry, sweaty, and smelly. Does his master size up his condition and say to him, "Go take a shower, and get something to eat"? No, not on your life. What he says is, "Go get those sweaty, smelly clothes off, take a shower, and then go into the kitchen and fix my dinner. And don't you take a bit of food until I have finished eating." Perhaps, the master even posts a guard to see that his orders are followed.

Now here is this servant throwing golden lumps of butter into a pot of mashed potatoes. There are the green peas bubbling on the stove, and the aroma of roast beef is filling the air. Can't you see him? There he stands, his own stomach growling, his mouth watering, but he can't touch a bite of the food. By the time he brings the food out, it doesn't even look like food anymore. It looks like mountains of potatoes, lakes of gravy, fields of green peas, and forests of roast beef reaching into the sky. And he has to stand there, with a towel hanging over one arm, waiting for his master to finish toying with the last pea on the end of his fork. Then he has to bring in the dessert! But instead of dessert, it looks like Niagaras of whipped cream cascading over cliffs of apricots!

OK, got the picture so far? Now think about it. Everything in that slave says, "Eat it yourself; forget what that guy out there has said." But he can't. He must obey his master—*against all his feelings.* He cannot say, "If I feel like it I will obey." And, Jesus makes the point that even then, he hasn't done anything exceptional, but only what he is supposed to do.

So, now three excuses have been demolished. You can't beg off from Christ's commands regarding forgiveness by simply saying, "When I get more faith," or by saying, "When I see the fruit," or by saying, "When I feel like it, I will forgive."

Don't Count on Your Feelings

"But, wait a minute! God doesn't want me to be a hypocrite, does He?"

No.

"Then, if I forgive someone when I don't feel like doing so, won't I be a hypocrite?"

No. Let me tell you why. The only reason you raise such an objection is because you have been influenced by the feeling-oriented times in which we live. You see, to think that way one must adopt an unbiblical, feeling-oriented view of hypocrisy. Your argument is that if you don't *feel* forgiving, granting another forgiveness will be insincere and thus hypocritical. But actually, you have bought into a very foolish viewpoint. Let me explain. Every morning I do something against all my feelings: I get up. Hardly ever do I want to get up. I'd like to throw the alarm clock through the window, cover my head with the covers, and forget the whole unpleasant business. But I don't. I get up. Now, does that make me a hypocrite? Of course not. And, that isn't the only thing I have to do against my feelings. All day long, in order to be responsible to God and others, I must do many things against my feelings. What does it mean when I pursue my responsibilities against my feelings? It simply means I am being responsible.

The biblical view of hypocrisy makes sense. If I had told you or led you to believe that I love to get out of bed in the morning when the truth is I don't, then I would have been acting hypocritically. But I've told you the truth.

"Well...I can see that, but something still seems wrong."

Perhaps that's because you're still holding on to a feeling-oriented view of forgiveness. But we saw in the last chapter that forgiveness is not a feeling but a promise. Now do you see how important that fact is? Let's explore it a bit further. Is Lewis Smedes right when he says,"...nor can one truly forgive out of duty"?[3]

The Promise of Forgiveness

You can make a promise whether or not you feel like it, and you can keep it whether or not you feel like it. You are in church, for example. The pastor is bearing down on husbands who are inconsiderate of their wives. He asks, "When was it you last took your wife out for dinner?" You think, *Let's see. Was it in September or March of 1978?* So, he gets under you fingernails; you are convicted. You don't feel like going out to eat, but you know you should. It's your "duty." So, on the way home you say, "Honey, I'm going to take you out for dinner Friday night." You didn't feel like it, but you did it. See, you can make a promise whether or not you feel like it. You *can* truly forgive out of duty.

When Jesus says, "You have simply done what you *ought to* have done" (Luke 17:10b), He is talking about *duty*. Smedes is wrong.

Now imagine that your Sunday promise of dinner out is followed by the worst week in history. Everything that could go wrong at work does. It is now Friday. You can't wait to get home—to relax, put your feet up, and enjoy home cooking. You have forgotten your promise. As you walk up to the front door, you can almost smell the evening meal that always greets you! But when you open the door, your wife meets you, fully clothed, and in her right mind! Suddenly, you are in yours. The last thing you feel like doing is going out to eat, but you will—or no meal! You see, you can also *keep* a promise whether or not you feel like it.

Gout? Of course. Rheumatism and gout. But that's why Jesus warned you at the outset.

Christian, is there someone you have refused to forgive? Someone who stepped on your toes whom you have never sought out? Do you have unfinished business to attend to? Then take this chapter to heart and by the grace of God go. Seek forgiveness yourself for your sin of refusal

[24]

or putting off reconciliation. Then talk about those matters that stand between you and resolve them God's way. Don't put it off any longer. Repent, ask God's forgiveness, and then go and do what Christ commands.

Refusal to forgive is a decision for vengeance. It is taking vengeance into your own hands. Joseph carried the logic of personal vengeance to its logical conclusion when, in response to his father's supposed plea for forgiveness, he said, "Don't be afraid; am I in God's place?" (Gen. 50:19) Because the Lord has said, "Vengeance is Mine; I will repay," to take vengeance of any kind—even the withholding of forgiveness—is an attempt to arrogate God's work to oneself.

When you say, "I forgive you" to another, you make a promise to him. It is a threefold promise. You promise not to remember his sin by not bringing it up to him, to others, or to yourself. The sin is buried. That promise is sometimes easier to make than to keep. I will devote an entire chapter to that problem of keeping the threefold promise of forgiveness later on. But for now, two things may help: First, remember how many times each day Jesus forgives you. Second, if you've really forgiven, it isn't the seventh time, it isn't the fifth. It isn't even the second. It is always the first.

3 *FORGIVENESS IS CONDITIONAL*

❧❧❧❧❧❧❧❧❧❧❧❧❧❧❧❧❧❧❧❧❧❧❧❧❧

What if the other person won't seek forgiveness or, after having been confronted with his or her sin, refuses to confess it? I have alluded to the problem in the last chapter, but here we must come to grips with the question in greater depth.

Today many Christian leaders erroneously teach that we must forgive another, even when that person clearly does not intend to seek forgiveness. For instance, David Augsburger writes: "Christ's way was the way of giving forgiveness even before asked, and even when it was not or never would be asked for by another."

As evidence for this astounding statement, he cites Christ's prayer, "Father, forgive them for they know not what they do" (Luke 23:34). Augsberger continues, "To think that we needn't forgive until we are asked is a myth to be punctured!"[4]

We shall consider these extraordinary statements in due time. But for now, listen to some others. In her book *Set Free*, Betty Tapscott is so insistent that we must "forgive unconditionally,"[5] that she teaches, "There are times when we may even have to forgive an animal."[6] She goes on to say, "Some people have to forgive an entire denomination...and an entire race of people" or an "entire country."[7]

Obviously, you cannot rebuke an animal hoping that it will confess sin and repent, or even an entire denomination, race, or country. Tapscott is talking about a forgiveness unknown to biblical writers who never so much as hint at anything of the sort. That there is something important here that she is trying to deal with is true, but her ideas not only seem farfetched, they run counter to the very idea of forgiveness itself, properly understood as a promise made to another.

Describing Kenneth McAll's practice, Roger Hurding writes, "here there is the idea of a 'double forgiveness' in which the patient willingly forgives dead relatives...and, at the same time, asks forgiveness from them....McAll sees Jesus Christ as the mediator of this two-way reconciliation."[8] In this system, it is apparent that the forgiveness of absent persons has been extended so far that McAll recommends not only prayers to the dead but, it would seem, also a form of spiritism.

Finally, in a doctoral dissertation dealing with the forgiveness of one's parents, the writer states, "The forgiving act does not need the actual presence of the parents. The patient, verbally, addresses the forgiveness to the imagined present parent."[9]

These examples are typical of various strains of Christian teaching abroad in the church that affect many people. They all deal with real problems, but in an unbiblical way. I could easily multiply examples but, there's no doubt, you have already experienced one or more manifestations of these ideas in your contacts with other Christians. Interestingly, the idea of forgiveness without repentance has become so widespread that it is now adopted by non-Christians as well.

Christ's Prayer on the Cross

Let's begin by considering Augsburger's statements about Jesus' prayer for the forgiveness of those who crucified Him. Was that prayer really an instance of a forgiveness "given...even before asked" and "even when it was not or never would be asked by the other?" Is he wise in wanting to "puncture" what he calls the "myth" that "we needn't forgive until we are asked"?

If, indeed, Jesus unconditionally forgave those who crucified Him, then, of course, that would mean that they had been forgiven without hearing or believing the Gospel. Clearly that teaching is heretical, and Augsburger cannot have thought through its implications very carefully. Surely he does not wish to say that Christ forgave people out of the blue, apart from the hearing of faith (Rom. 10:14ff). On the other hand, if Christ had really prayed the prayer Augsburger describes, it would have been a prayer that contradicted all of Scripture and, incidentally, a prayer that failed.

On the cross, Jesus did not forgive; He prayed. The same is true of Stephen. If forgiveness is unconditional, Jesus, Stephen, and others would have *forgiven* their murderers rather than use what, if true, would be a roundabout way to do so. At other times Jesus had no hesitancy in saying, "Your sins be forgiven you." No, contrary to Augsburger's claims, the saying from the cross was not a statement of forgiveness (unconditional or not) but a prayer. The reference to the cross is, in a sense, irrelevant since it was not a case of forgiveness at all.

How can Christ's words best be explained?

Well, we don't want to say Christ prayed an unscriptural prayer—that is bedrock. Then in some sense we must recognize that the prayer was legitimate. Since Jesus said to the Father, "I knew that You always hear [heed] Me" (John 11:42), we believe also that His prayer was answered. How could that be? Not apart from the means, but *by* them.

[28]

Jesus' prayer was answered in the response to the preaching of Peter and the apostles on the day of Pentecost, and on those other occasions when thousands of Jews repented and believed the Gospel (Acts 2:37-38; 3:17-19; 4:4). They were not forgiven the sin of crucifying the Saviour apart from believing that He was dying for their sins, but precisely by doing so in response to the faithful preaching of the Gospel in Jerusalem. We do not have to resort to some strange doctrine of the forgiveness of sins apart from faith in Christ in order to explain Christ's prayer.

So, it is clear that the forgiveness for which Christ prayed was not unconditional but depended entirely on faith in the very act in which He was engaged at the time He prayed. How unthinkable it is that Christ could be undergoing the sufferings of the Cross, dying for the sins of His people so as to forgive them, and at that very time ask for forgiveness by some other means! When men teach doctrines that are unbiblical, they get into trouble with other biblical teachings as well and are forced to interpret the Scriptures in an unorthodox manner. The so-called "myth" that Augsburger wants to puncture turns out to be the very truth of God.

What About Parents, Cats, Countries, and Whole Churches?

Obviously, Betty Tapscott's views are foreign to the Bible. While we are commanded to forgive others, we never read anything about forgiving animals or masses of people whom we are unable to rebuke, whose confession of sin we could never hear, or to whom we could not make the promise "not to remember" their sin against them. It is a forgiveness very different from God's forgiveness that Tapscott teaches. Indeed, as one peruses her book, it becomes clear that her major concern is about *what forgiveness does for the one who forgives*, not how it pleases God or shows love to others. That same self-oriented emphasis lies behind

many extraordinary measures such as talking to the dead, forgiving parents whose presence is "imagined" (Velazquez-Garcia), and "forgiving" large groups of people who are totally oblivious to it.

Any Truth in All of This?

Yes, there is a truth that is greatly misunderstood and misrepresented. It is found in one passage that (rightly) deals with the problem of forgiving when the one to be forgiven is either not present or unwilling to confess sin. It is found in Mark 11:25, "And when you stand praying, if you have something against anyone, forgive him, so that your Father in heavens also may forgive you your trespasses."

Here a nice distinction must be made. As we have seen, when God forgives us, He goes on record declaring that He will remember our sins no more. That is the *granting* of forgiveness by which He promises never again to use our sinful record against us. Forgiveness, however, *does* something, as we saw in chapter one. It lifts the guilt from the shoulders of another allowing reconciliation to occur. We must discuss reconciliation more fully later on, but in this verse Jesus is concerned about the attitude of the believer as he stands before God in prayer. If he is inwardly unwilling to forgive his brother or sister, he cannot expect forgiveness from the Father. Thus, preceding the *promise* (or *granting*) of forgiveness to another, one must prepare to lift that guilt so that the promise he makes, even if against his feelings, will be sincerely meant and kept. He may not simply repeat a formula; he must forgive from his heart.[10] Like his Heavenly Father, by prayer, the believer seeks to become *"ready to forgive"* (Ps. 86:5, MLB). That is the meaning of Mark 11:25.

Notice that in prayer one does not "pretend" to forgive another, nor does he commune with the dead. What he does is express *to God* his genuine concern to be reconciled to his brother (if possible) and his willingness to grant forgiveness to him. His prayer is to God, and since he is not granting God forgiveness, in the verse the word "forgive" must be used by extension to express the willingness to forgive another. Perhaps it means even more. Possibly it implies a prayer, modeled after Christ's prayer, that God will also forgive the offender (again, not apart from, but through the means). Certainly, we can be sure of this much, that it is a prayer to take all resentment and bitterness from the heart of the supplicant.

It is also clear that this "forgiving" in prayer in no way exempts one from granting forgiveness to his brother. Misuse of this verse affords an easy way out for those who do not want to face the rheumatism and gout mentioned in the previous chapter.

Commenting on Mark 11:25 (in *An American Commentary*), Clarke says, "Prayer is a tremendous power, but it cannot be used for the gratification of personal resentments." It may be that after cursing the fig tree (not an act of personal resentment, but a symbolic act of Jesus as Messiah toward unrepentant Israel), and His words on the power of prayer, which precede this verse, Jesus wanted to distinguish the personal act from the official one, so that no one would get the idea that he could use prayer as a means of cursing others out of personal vengeance. Whatever may be said about why this verse appears where it does, it is clear that it gives no support to any of the strange views set forth above.

Church Discipline

In Matthew 18:15ff, Jesus sets forth an outline of the program of church discipline that He intends His church to follow. That program (for details see my book, *Handbook of Church Discipline*, Zondervan) basically moves forward in four steps:

> "If your brother sins against you, go and convict
> him of his sin privately, with just the two of you

present. If he listens to you, you have won your brother. But if he won't listen to you, take with you one or two others so that by the mouth of two or three witnesses every word may be confirmed. And if he refuses to listen to them, tell it to the church. And if he refuses to listen to the church, treat him like a Gentile and a tax collector. Let Me assure you that whatever you bind on earth shall have been bound in heaven, and whatever you loose on earth shall have been loosed in heaven. Again, I tell you that if two of you agree on earth about anything they ask, it will be done for them by My Father in the heavens. Where two or three meet together in My Name, I am there among them." (Matt. 18:15-20)

As you can see, the brother sinned against goes to his brother (just as we have seen in Luke 17:3). If there is confession and forgiveness, the matter is settled right there and must go no further. Reconciliation occurs. If the sinning brother refuses to hear his brother, the latter must return with one or two others to act first as counselors, and if there is still no repentance, to act at the next step as witnesses. Again, if they are successful and forgiveness occurs, the matter stops right there. But if they fail to convince the recalcitrant brother to repent, the matter is formally taken before the church. If there is repentance and forgiveness, the matter stops there. But if even that extreme measure fails, then the offender is put out of the church and treated as a pagan and tax collector (both of whom were out of the church). Does anything in that process sound even remotely consonant with the statement of Minirth and Meier that *we must forgive no matter what response* we get from the other person"?[11]

Now, notice how on failure to bring about repentance, forgiveness, and reconciliation, more and more persons (two alone, one or two others in addition, the whole church and, finally, the world itself) become involved in the process.

If forgiveness were unconditional, then this entire process of discipline would be impossible. It is my contention that the very existence of such a program as this *requires* us to believe that forgiveness is conditional. Consider the following.

If we were to grant forgiveness to a brother apart from his repentance and desire for forgiveness, then why bother with the process? One would simply say, "I forgive you" and walk away. The whole point of the progressive nature of Christ's program of discipline is that where there is no repentance, increasingly larger efforts must be made to bring it about. The matter cannot be dropped simply by saying, "I forgive you, whether you repent or not." God is not interested in forgiveness as an end in itself, or as a therapeutic technique that benefits the one doing the forgiving. He wants reconciliation to take place, and that can only be brought about by repentance.

Since the program does exist, is commanded by Christ, and He promises to work by it to resolve personal problems (see v. 18-20; v. 18 is no warrant for small prayer meetings), *we must reckon with it.* We dare not ignore it because of some programs we wish to follow instead. The reason that the process of church discipline is so pertinent to the present discussion is this: *No Christian may ever make a promise that will keep him from obeying a clear command of Christ.*

If we are to forgive brothers and sisters purely on our own, apart from any whisper of repentance, in doing so, we promise them not to bring the matter up again—to them, to others, or to ourselves. Yet, that is exactly what the process of church discipline requires us to do—bring it up, again and again and again, to them and to others, until repentance and reconciliation are effected or the rebellious brother is evicted from the church.

God's Forgiveness

It should go without saying that since our forgiveness is modeled after God's (Eph. 4:32), it must be conditional. Forgiveness by God rests on clear, unmistakable conditions. The apostles did not merely announce that God had forgiven men, who should acknowledge and rejoice in the fact but, rather, they were sent forth to preach "*repentance* and the forgiveness of sins" (Luke 24:47; Acts 17:30). The sins of those who repented and trusted in the Saviour as the One who shed His blood for them were forgiven *on the conditions of repentance and faith*. Paul and the apostles turned away from those who refused to meet the conditions, just as John and Jesus did earlier when the scribes and the Pharisees would not repent.

Every Offense?

"But," you ask, *"must one go to another about every offense? Must there be rebuking, repenting and forgiving over everything that happens? Why, a husband and wife would hardly be able to keep lists of all the matters they have to deal with, let alone get around to doing so."*

A good question. No. God has provided a means for handling the multitude of offenses that we commit against one another. But it is not by forgiveness. In 1 Peter 4:8, quoting Proverbs 17:9, Peter points out that those who love one another "cover a multitude of sins" in love. It is only those sins which throw the covers off that must be dealt with by the Luke 17 and Matthew 18 processes: those offenses that break fellowship and lead to an unreconciled condition require forgiveness. Otherwise, we simply learn to overlook a multitude of offenses against ourselves, recognizing that we are all sinners and that we must gratefully thank others for covering our sins as well.

Smedes cannot be right when he divides offenses into categories, some of which must be forgiven and some that need not be.[12] Any offense, no matter what its nature, may create an unreconciled condition, depending on how the offended party responds to the offense. The same offense may or may not result in an unreconciled condition, depending on many changeable and unpredictable factors, such as the predisposition of the one offended, his past experiences, the number of times it has been repeated, how he interprets it, and so on. Categorized lists of offenses, therefore, are misleading and unhelpful.

Of course, it is possible to rationalize here. I may say (and perhaps even convince myself for a time) that I have covered a brother's sin when I by no means have done so. It is important to become scrupulously honest with oneself without becoming overly scrupulous. If you have troubles with this, you should talk to your pastor or to some mature Christian about the problem.

"But what do you do about forgiving the dead or others with whom you have lost touch?"

Certainly, you must not pray to the dead. Nor should you act out some charade by imagining you are talking to them. Since such people cannot repent and seek forgiveness from you, you cannot grant forgiveness to them. In prayer you may simply tell God of your desire to forgive and your determination to rid your heart of all bitterness and resentment toward them. That is all you can do and all you need to do. Those Christians who died before reconciliation have now been glorified and made perfect. They don't need your forgiveness. Glorification has made them the sort of people you would so delight to be around that, doubtless, on meeting them you would forget their offenses. Those with whom you have lost touch may cross your path again. At such a later time you can finally deal with matters as you should have earlier.

When wronged by countries (e.g., Nazi Germany) or denominations, rather than going through a mock exercise called "forgiveness," you must follow the example of dying saints (Acts 7:60) who, in imitation of their Lord, pray for the forgiveness of their persecutors. In response God

may be pleased to bring many of the group to repentance leading to forgiveness.

What shall we say then? It is clear that forgiveness— promising another never to bring up his offense again to use it against him—is conditioned on the offender's willingness to confess it as sin and to seek forgiveness.[13] You are not obligated to forgive an unrepentant sinner, but you are obligated to try to bring him to repentance. All the while you must entertain a genuine hope and willingness to forgive the other and a desire to be reconciled to him or her. Because this biblical teaching runs counter to much teaching in the modern church, it is important to understand it. Such forgiveness is modeled after God's forgiveness which is unmistakably conditioned on repentance and faith.

FORGIVENESS AFTER FORGIVENESS

Perhaps the best summary of the problems addressed in the previous chapter is the description by G.K. Chesterton of a man who "was so anxious to forgive that he denied the need of forgiveness."[14] Though this may sound like a paradox, Chesterton is describing a person to whom forgiveness becomes so superficial and sentimental that he no longer sees a need for true, biblical forgiveness.

Broadus, commenting on Matthew 6:12 (*An American Commentary*), refers to the same difficulty but puts it somewhat differently. "But, like many terms expressive of Christian duty, the word forgive has come to be often used in a weakened sense, and many anxious minds are misled by its ambiguity."[15] Because of shallow thinking, trying to find an easier way around the rheumatism and gout, or just plain misunderstanding, many erroneous ideas regarding forgiveness have been entertained. In this chapter our task is to clear away another, thereby enabling us to get at the precious truth that lies hidden behind it.

Put simply, the problem is this: How can there be forgiveness after forgiveness? If you have been forgiven once and for all by faith in Jesus Christ, why is there any need for forgiveness from God or others afterward? Why not

say whenever you sin, "Thank You, Lord, that it's all under the blood!" and go your way? How can there be a need for continued repentance and forgiveness when God has promised not to remember those sins against you again?

In his provocative book *Truth vs Tradition*, Howard Hart writes, "In the context of New Testament Scripture, the concept of the necessity of the confession of one's sins to God for forgiveness, as a believer, cannot be found."[16]

In that chapter, Hart is discussing 1 John 1:9 and, in a totally convincing argument, shows that the traditional interpretation is in error. The verse does not speak of regular confession by believers but of those who are identified as believers because they have confessed or made a profession of the fact that they are sinners. (Indeed, he even might have strengthened his case by noting how John used the word *confess* elsewhere, as in 1 John 4:2-3.) But on the main point he is in error. Believers are required to confess to God and others in repentance in order to receive forgiveness. There are verses that Hart does not consider.

Listen to these:

> And forgive us our debts *as we also have forgiven our debtors*...Now if you forgive people their trespasses against you, so too your Heavenly Father will forgive you, but if you won't forgive people, *neither will you Father forgive your trespasses*. (Matt. 6:12, 14-15)

Unmistakably, the Lord's Prayer (a prayer Christ gave His disciples as a model for daily prayer) structures into it confession of sin leading to forgiveness. The only element in the Lord's Prayer on which Jesus comments further, as a sort of footnote (vv. 14-15), is this one about forgiveness. This fact not only emphasizes the need for forgiveness but in the commentary on the forgiveness clause in the Lord's Prayer, makes the point that communication with the Father suffers whenever there is a refusal to reestablish communication with a brother or sister through forgiveness.

The same point in nearly the same words is found in Mark 11:25, a verse we have already had occasion to notice in another regard, "And when you stand praying, if you have something against anyone, forgive him, so that your Father in the heavens also may forgive you your trespasses."

Of course, there is also Luke 6:36-37, "Be merciful as your Father is merciful. Don't judge and you won't be judged; don't condemn and you won't be condemned; forgive and you will be forgiven."

In 1 Peter 3:7, Peter exhorts husbands, "Live with your wives in an understanding way [literally, "according to knowledge"]...*so that your prayers may not be interrupted.*" Again, the failure of believing husbands to communicate properly with their wives hinders communication with God. Obviously, if husbands have been failing in their role and fellowship with the Father is interrupted, the way to correct this is to repent and seek forgiveness from their wives and be reconciled to them.

Daniel, a righteous man, was not wrong in confessing his sins as well as those of the people to His Heavenly, Father (Dan. 9:20), was he? The Israelites, likewise, surely were correct in confessing their sins (Neh. 9:2), as , indeed, was Ezra (Ezra 9:5ff; 10:1). And certainly it would be a mistake to ignore the exhortations in James 5:15-16 and 1 Corinthians 11:31. In both of these passages sin by unrepentant believers gets in the way of a proper relationship with God.

What the writer of Proverbs 28:13 had to say still holds good. "He who conceals his transgressions will not prosper, but he who confesses and forsakes them will receive mercy" (MLB).[4]

The New Testament word *confess* means "to say the same thing." Thus it may be used to express agreement

with a truth (as in 1 John where one professes agreement with the fact that Christ came in the flesh) or it may be used to express agreement with God when He says a given attitude, thought, or behavior is sinful. In the latter sense it is used of one who acknowledges his sin.

Just as it is wrong to confuse the two, as Hart has so carefully observed about 1 John 1:9 (a passage we shall not depend on in this chapter), so it is equally incorrect to dismiss passages in which confession of sin by believers is either described or mentioned as such.

How May the Problem Be Resolved?

That there is a problem with forgiveness after forgiveness is clear. But the way to resolve the problem is not to slight or deny either the truth that we have been forgiven once for all by God or the equally clear truth that believers must continue to be forgiven by Him. How may this seeming contradiction be resolved?

God deals with men both as Judge and as Father. Human beings are born relating to Him only as Creator and Judge. They are not born a part of His redeemed family. As unforgiven sinners they stand condemned to everlasting punishment. When, therefore, they hear the Gospel and trust Christ as Saviour, He forgives their sins once and for all *as Judge*. At the same time, they receive the right to become God's children (John 1:12). Thereafter they also relate to Him *as Father*.

In His two relationships to believers, God relates differently. As Judge, He looks at the record; it is spotless because their sin—all of it—is forgiven (remembered against them no more), and in its place is recorded the perfect record of Jesus Christ. It is this judicial side of the relationship that is completed, once and for all.

But as Father, God has much yet to do to train believers to become obedient children. The very fact that He disciplines them is evidence that they are true children (Heb.

[40]

12:7-11). He is making His children holy (Heb. 12:10b). Part of this training of His children involves their sin. While He doesn't throw sinning believers out of the family, the Father does discipline them for their sins for their benefit. He expects them as loving children to repent, confess sins, and receive His forgiveness. The important distinction to keep in mind is that there is both judicial forgiveness and parental forgiveness. The first is done and over with; the second is ongoing.

This is not a new idea. This idea was taught many years ago in the *Westminster Confession of Faith*: "God doth continue to forgive the sins of those who are justified...because they fall under His fatherly displeasure."[18] These writers long ago resolved the problem. It is amazing how, so often today, old issues are raised, but less-than-biblical responses are given. There seems to be little consideration of the way in which such issues were dealt with in the history of the church.

Is there Biblical Evidence for this Distinction?

Some biblical evidence for this distinction has been offered already from Hebrews. But once more consider the Lord's Prayer and the other passages that describe the confession and forgiveness of sins by believers. In the introduction to the Lord's Prayer, Jesus describes the believer as praying "Our Father." The prayer is a prayer for the child of God; it may not be offered (rightly) by any other. Moreover, in Jesus' footnote to the petition concerning forgiveness (Matt. 6:14-15), the word "Father" is used twice: "So too your Heavenly Father will forgive you...neither will your Father forgive your trespasses."

In Mark 11:25, we read, "So that your Father in the heavens also may forgive you your trespasses." And, immediately prior to the words in Luke 6:37, "Forgive and you will be forgiven," Jesus says, "Be merciful as your Father is merciful."

It should be evident, then, that to distinguish between judicial forgiveness (dealt with once and for all in justification by faith) and parental forgiveness is a biblical construct. Jesus' regular use of the word Father in the contexts in which He emphasizes the need for parental forgiveness seems not merely incidental but deliberate.

At any rate, it is clear that the Scriptures themselves speak of forgiveness after forgiveness, and consider it the most natural thing in the world for a Father to condition His willingness to extend His parental forgiveness on the right attitudes of His children toward other members of the family.

What Is It All About?

Well, we have seen already that God is concerned to discipline His children in order to make them holy. Clearly, the withholding of forgiveness from a child who himself withholds it from another is a disciplinary measure, carried out for the good of the entire family. It is not that God does not want to forgive; the very passages quoted are all an incentive for believing children to forgive *so that God may quickly forgive them.* That is certainly uppermost in the passages considered. However, there is more than this to understand.

When you must forgive another who has wronged you, before confessing your own sin to God, this very fact helps you to recognize how heinous your sin is to God. In thinking through the condition you are compelled to think of the sin against you and say, "I too am like that person who wronged me." Did he besmirch your name? Well, you have done the same to God's name. Was he ungrateful to you? How ungrateful have you been to God? It is a salutary thing when confessing sin to God, not merely to approach Him in a casual manner abut your sin, but also to see that you have wronged him as seriously as (or far worse than) you have been wronged.

Along with the benefit of being brought to the place where you think about the seriousness of your sins, as Luke 6:35 and Ephesians 4:32 indicate, coupling one's own forgiveness with that of his brother tends to develop mercy and tenderheartedness in the one who prays. The person who comes to prayer recognizing his need for forgiveness from the Father is required to think also of his brother's need for forgiveness. In effect it is one form of coming to love your neighbor *as yourself.* God wants to build a capacity for compassion in His children.

Finally, a person who has a heart that is filled with vengeance, bitterness, or resentment isn't ready for forgiveness, because he is holding onto these sins, refusing to confess and forsake them. From every perspective, then, you can see that God has structured forgiveness in a way that tends for the good of all His children.

Rather than consider confession of sin to God and granting of forgiveness as a burden, then, Christians ought to rejoice that with God "there is forgiveness" (Ps. 130:4). It is an untold blessing to have a forgiving Father as one's God. Buddhists, for instance, must try to content themselves with this statement: "Not in the sky, not in the midst of the sea, not if we enter into the clefts of the mountains, is there known a spot in the whole world where a man might be freed from an evil deed" (*Dhammapada* 9:9).[19]

Islam has 99 names for God, but not one of them is "Father." Yet, your God has compassion on you "as a father has compassion for his children" (Ps. 103:13). The Word of God affirms that He is "merciful" and forgave the sins of His people (Ps. 78:38). Praise Him, and rejoice that provision is made for drawing near to the Father in prayerful confession.

What about Matthew 18:21-35?

Then Peter came and said to Him, "Lord when my brother sins against me, how many times should

I forgive him? As many as seven times?"

Then Jesus said to him, "I don't tell you seven times but seventy times seven!

"Therefore, the empire from the heavens is like a king who wanted to settle accounts with his slaves, and as he began settlement, one was brought to him who owed him ten thousand talents. And since he couldn't repay the debt, the lord commanded that he, his wife, his children, and everything that he owned be sold to repay the debt

"The servant fell on his knees and begged him, 'Be patient with me and I'll repay you everything.'

"And the lord took pity on his slave and released him and forgave the loan.

"But when he went out that same slave found one of his fellow slaves who owed him one hundred denarii, and he seized him and throttled him, saying, 'Repay whatever you owe.'

"So his fellow slave fell down and begged him, 'Be patient with me and I'll repay you.'

"But he wouldn't. Instead, he went and threw him into prison until he paid the debt.

"When his other fellow slaves saw what had happened, they were greatly upset and went and told their lord all about what had taken place.

"Then his lord called him and said to him: 'You wicked slave, I forgave you your entire debt because you begged me. Shouldn't you also have shown mercy to your fellow slave as I showed mercy to you?'

"And his lord became angry, and handed him over to the torturers until he paid his entire debt.

"So also will My Heavenly Father do to you unless each of you forgives his brother from his heart."

This parable is the story form of the truth with which we have been dealing in Matthew 6:14-15, Mark 11:25, and Luke 6:37. But verses 34-35 seem to take on a far more somber cast. How can they be explained?

Clearly, spoken to Peter, (v. 21), and directed to the disciples in general (18:1, 21) the parable has to do with believers and forgiveness after forgiveness. It is impossible to relate the parable merely to unbelievers and thus explain away the tortures (v. 34), etc. How, then, can it be related to a merciful Heavenly Father disciplining His children through forgiveness?

Some of the parables, which are true-to-life stores, have bad characters in them—the dishonest steward, the widow and the judge, the selfish householder—doing in the parable exactly what they would do in real life. Neither the characters nor the things they say or do are to be emulated. Jesus' materials are drawn from real life and depict it as those around Him knew it. The parables, moreover, are not allegories in which every feature is paralleled with some point that is being made. Some of the details, therefore, are there simply to make the parable hold together as a story, and serve no other function. Ordinarily, only one major point is made (here, in the form of a question, v. 33). The parable humbles us whenever we are reluctant to forgive another by stressing three things:

1. *The unreasonableness of our attitude.* We, who have been forgiven so much by God (some $10 million in the parable) refuse to forgive a small debt (possibly $20) in another. In doing so, we are like the Pharisee who loved little because he was forgiven little, rather than like the woman who loved much because she was forgiven much (Luke 7:36-47).

2. *The meanness of such an attitude.* How could a person just forgiven so much refuse to forgive another so little? The very grossness of the compari-

son, intended by our Lord, puts the matter in its exact light. We have been forgiven more than we could even imagine in our justification. Ought we not, therefore, be most grateful and out of great gratitude be moved to extend forgiveness to those who, by comparison, commit but trifling sins against us even when done 70 times 7?

3. *The danger of such an unforgiving spirit.* God will not overlook it. If the kings calls his servant to account, will not the Father (note the use of this word in v. 35) do the same?

"But what of the torturers?" you ask. *"And what of paying the last cent?"*

First, many interpreters make the word "torturers" simply equivalent to jailers of a rude sort. If true, that softens the situation somewhat. However, it really solves no problem: in the parable the king revokes the forgiven servant's pardon. According to Romans 11:29, along with a multitude of other passages, we are shown how it is impossible for a person once saved to be lost and suffer eternal punishment. Therefore, the conclusion of the parable must be understood in some other way.

Some ease their way out of the problem by claiming this speaks not of true believers but of those who make a false profession of faith, who *claim* to be forgiven, and who, by their unforgiving attitudes, demonstrate that they never were. The conclusion of the parable, therefore, refers to eternal judgment in hell. But that escape seems too easy. Christ was speaking to His disciples; He was specifically answering a question by Peter. He was referring to forgiving "brothers" and distinctly makes a point of how great a forgiveness the servant had received.

We must refer the parable to believers, just as the similar statements in Matthew 6 and elsewhere clearly refer to them. In doing so, the revocation of forgiveness must not be pressed, as though Christians could lose their salvation, any more than the idea of literal torture should be emphasized. What Jesus is saying (and He stresses that He and the Father are in agreement in this by calling Him "*My Father*") is that, in one way or another God will remind the believer who forgets the magnitude of God's grace in forgiving him so much.

The Caspar Milquestoast mentality of many avant-garde Christians today revolts against any idea of harsh punishment by the Father toward His sons. Yet, the passages in Hebrews 12 and 1 Corinthians 11 already mentioned demonstrate that God does not lightly brush off the sins of the saints. There is much false teaching today in this regard. Perhaps, it is directed no more fully elsewhere than toward the stern warnings given to the Christian who refuses to forgive.

Forgiveness after forgiveness, then, is an important matter that must be rightly understood. Your careful attention to such matters will not go unrewarded. Closer fellowship to your Heavenly Father and to your brothers and sisters in Christ, as well as the fostering of greater unity in your church, will be the inevitable results.

5 WHEN YOU ARE THE OFFENDER

There are times when even the most sincere Christians find themselves at odds with others. Often it is not their fault. Then, if the offense is not one that may be covered in love, it is necessary to pursue the route charted in Luke 17:3ff. If reconciliation does not occur, next one must employ the process of church discipline outlined in Matthew 18:15ff. That much is clear. But what of the time when *you* are the offender and do not want to be reconciled to a brother or sister? That is the subject of this brief chapter.

The first thing that must be said is that you place yourself in jeopardy. You are in danger of church discipline, and even worse, your intransigence will strain your relationship to your Heavenly Father. Since I have already commented on both of these matters from the perspective of the one offended, you already know what, if anything, will happen as a result. If your brother or sister fails to approach you in accord with Luke 17 or Matthew 18, as is likely in a church that seldom follows the directions of her Lord, you may think that you can get away with your stubbornness. But, if for a time you do, you put yourself in an even more dangerous position than if he instituted church discipline against you. It means a longer period of poor relations with the Father in which it is likely that you will not only become hardened to your sin but, in justifying it, only enlarge the offense. And, as we shall see, it means God, your Father, may judge you.

Do Something Quickly

That is why Jesus emphasized the importance of quickly coming to an agreement with your opponent and even interrupting an act of worship when necessary in order to be reconciled. Here are His words:

> "So then, if you are offering your gift at the altar, and there remember that your brother has something against you, leave your gift right there in front of the altar, and go first and be reconciled to your brother; then come and offer your gift. Quickly come to terms with your legal opponent, while you are with him on the way; otherwise your opponent may hand you over to the judge, and the judge to his officer, and you will be thrown into prison. Let me assure you that you surely will not get out of there until you have paid the last cent." (Matt. 5:23-26)

Two phrases stand out: "Go first" (v. 24) and "Quickly come to terms" (v. 25). Both of these phrases stress the urgency of reconciliation. The idea of "first" being reconciled before continuing an act of worship is striking. Not only is urgency stressed, but again, Jesus' words accord with what we saw in the last chapter. God insists you must be on good terms with your brothers and sisters if you expect to remain on good terms with Him. Your worship, if you have wronged another and not made it right with him

by confession and forgiveness, is unacceptable. First (don't miss the order of priority), before offering a gift to God, straighten matters out with your brother; the gift God really wants is reconciliation (Ps. 51:17).

The note of urgency appears not only here in the offering scene in which reconciliation takes precedence over worship and in the scenario about settling matters with a legal opponent on the way to court, it emerges again in such commands as, "Let not the sun go down on your wrath" (Eph. 4:26) and "Pursue [a strong word] peace with everybody" (Heb. 12:14).

Indeed, Paul mentions a powerful incentive for reconciliation in 1 Corinthians 11:31, "If we carefully judged ourselves, we wouldn't be judged." Corinthian Christians were acting in reprehensible ways that estranged them from one another. They were dividing into groups, using their gifts in selfish and unloving ways, and even (as this passage indicates) failing to show love to one another at the Lord's table (see vv. 18-22). Because they had not abandoned these sinful practices and come to reconciliation one with another, God Himself had begun to judge them by sending weakness, sickness, and even death (v. 30). In the midst of this discussion, Paul observed that such judgment by God was unnecessary. If they had judged themselves, God wouldn't have needed to judge them.

This is a strong warning. Those who will not quickly deal with their sins against one another will not get off scot-free even when an offended brother or sister fails to utilize church discipline, or a congregation refuses to exercise it. Under those circumstances, God Himself will act in judgment. It is better not to wait until that happens, says Paul. The thing to do is to carefully judge yourselves. By the words "judge yourselves," Paul certainly included dealing in a biblical manner with sins that you discover.

But What about Psalm 51:4?

In Psalm 51:4, David wrote, "Against Thee, Thee only have I sinned and done what is evil in Thy sight". If sin is against God *alone*, as David (who had murdered Uriah and committed adultery with Bathsheba) seems to affirm, why must there be confession to another who has been wronged? Isn't it enough to confess to God and seek His forgiveness?

All the passages adduced thus far in this book refute any such idea. Even if David's agonized exclamation cannot be explained to you with complete satisfaction, there is an overwhelming biblical witness to the need for confession to human beings and the need to be forgiven by and reconciled to them. The evidence is clear that all sin is sin against God, but also that much sin is also sin against man. The proper way to view the situation is the way Jesus proposes when He puts into the mouth of the prodigal son these words: "Father, I have sinned against heaven and before you" (Luke 15:18).

"But what, then, do David's words mean?"

That is good question. Two answers have been given. The first, that since Nathan's exposure of his sin, which, up until then, David had managed to keep quiet, had come with such a shocking intensity ("Thou art the man"), David (as the psalm shows) was overwhelmed with grief and could see nothing but the horrendous wrong he had done against God. It is this to which his words refer. Because he was so sensitive to his relationship to God, it was this and this alone that dominated his thought.

There is another interpretation that translates the verse "Before Thee, Thee only." That is to say, since the sin was done in secret (2 Sam. 12:12) God, and only God knew about it. David here is acknowledging that God, therefore, had sent Nathan, as His messenger to expose the sin he had kept under wraps and call him to repentance.

Whatever the best way to understand the verse, it is clear that in verse 14, where David refers to his bloodguiltiness, he acknowledges his wrong against Uriah.

One fact stands out. Whenever one sins against his brother, he has, thereby, sinned against God as well. There can never, therefore, be an occasion on which a Christian, obligated to confess sin to another and seek his forgiveness, is not also obligated to do the same toward God. Indeed, one of the ways in which he may possibly approach his brother, may be by assuring him that he has sought God's forgiveness and that he is now seeking his. But the two are bound up together. One cannot seek God's forgiveness, and intend later on to seek his brother's forgiveness if and when he gets around to it. He may not separate the two. In praying to God, he must express a genuine desire and intention to be reconciled to his brother. Otherwise, as we have seen, God is not willing to reestablish warm fatherly relationships.

The Matter of "Heart Sins"

Not all sins are outward transgressions against another. When Jesus spoke of committing adultery in the heart (Matt. 5:28), He was referring to what I am here calling a "heart sin." The heart sin is known only to God and the sinner. It is not known to the one toward whom the sinful thought in the heart is directed. Lust, anger, envy, etc., that flare up in the heart, but are dealt with before they are outwardly manifested, need not be confessed to anyone but God. Indeed, confession to persons totally unaware of what you are thinking can lead to additional sin and unnecessary hurt.

Heart sins must be carefully distinguished from other transgressions, unknown to other parties to whom you are obligated to confess and seek forgiveness. Consider this common scenario. A husband or wife has committed adultery. The fact is unknown to his or her spouse. The affair is called off, the sinner is repentant, and wants to know what his or her responsibilities toward the spouse are. Many (wrongly) advise, "Don't tell your spouse. If you do, you will only cause more trouble and heartache. What she or he doesn't know won't hurt."

David Augsburger says he once advised a man not to tell his wife about an affair:

> "Then don't," I suggested.
> "You mean I don't have to tell her about it to find forgiveness?"
> "Well that all depends on you. If you can accept God's forgiveness and trust Him with your guilt feelings, maybe you won't need to open it up to her to get relief."[20]

This is poor advice. At first it may seem the kind and compassionate thing to do. And, of course, it is easy to talk oneself into believing so. But consider the facts: Unlike a heart sin, there has been a distinct act of transgression against one's spouse. "But she isn't aware of it," you protest. True—and false. There is no human relationship so close as the "one flesh" relationship of marriage. Indeed, in discussing this in Ephesians 5, Paul says that whatever a husband does for his wife he does for himself (vv. 28-31). When the sexual relationship has been violated, therefore, you can be sure that there will be an impact on the marriage. You just can't have a third party come between two who are one flesh without that happening.

Now it is possible that the other party will not know that adultery has taken place, but the other party will surely sense that something is wrong. Perhaps the innocent party will even think that he or she has been the one who is at fault. Thus, there has been sin that affects another, even when that other person is unaware of the exact cause of the strain in the marriage.

Moreover, there are all sorts of ways in which the fact of adultery may become known at a later point in time. Now when repentance is warm is the time to deal with the sin, not months or years later. And it is better to confess on your own initiative than to do so only after being found out. Reconciliation is easier under those circumstances because confession itself is an evident sign of repentance.

Indeed how genuine is the repentance if one fails to deal with the problem? Is there a real concern for full reconciliation? Is there a desire to resolve other problems in the relationship that may have led to the sin? These are important questions that cannot be brushed aside. And what of the guilty one? What kind of free future relationship can he have with his spouse when all the while, hanging over his head, is the possibility of exposure?

No, the sin must be revealed. But my strong advice is to take with you a mature Christian or a pastor who will be on hand to pick up the pieces when the secret is disclosed and who will be available for regular counseling in days immediately ahead, to put the marriage together again in a new and better way. I have seen innumerable marriages that were stronger after the weld than before the break when confession and subsequent counseling were carried out judiciously.

Taking the First Step

What more can I say? If you are the offender who has brought about a rift in a relationship between yourself and another—whether it be a family member, a spouse, a friend, or a church member—you are obligated to go. And you must go quickly. When you go, however, do not go justifying your sin. ("I've come to tell you I'm sorry about what I said after you pulled that rotten trick on me.") No, stick entirely to your own sin. Otherwise, your repentance may not seem genuine. Indeed, you can get so caught up in this sort of thing that the attempt at reconciliation can turn again into another offense that will make it all the harder to achieve reconciliation in the end. Stick strictly to what you have done wrong. Later on, if there are offenses against you that you want to get cleared up, you can talk to the brother or sister about them. And you can talk from a point of strength rather than weakness. Your own transgressions will have been buried never again to be exhumed.

If you are convicted by what you have read, then by all means, before some extraneous occurrence sweeps it from your mind and you grow cold again, make an appointment to see the one you have wronged to seek his or her forgiveness. Whenever possible, meet at a place where you will not be disturbed by children, telephones, and other interruptions. Deal with the issue there. Don't try to handle a matter as important as this on the run (e.g., as you happen to pass the other person in the hall at church between Sunday School and the morning worship service). Restaurants and other public places are usually good because people rarely blow up or yell in the presence of others near at hand.

Go, brother or sister. Go. Pick up the phone now.

6 OTHER ERRORS CONCERNING FORGIVENESS

ɔɑɪɔɑɪɔɑɪɔɑɪɔɑɪɔɑɪɔɑɪɔɑɪɔɑɪɔɑɪɔɑɪɔɑɪɔɑɪɔɑɪɔɑɪɔɑɪɔɑɪɔɑɪɔɑɪ

It is probably because forgiveness is such an important matter that so many errors have crept into the thinking of the church about it. It is not pleasant but certainly necessary to expose these. Otherwise, Christians will go on attempting unnecessary, or even impossible, tasks like trying to "forget."

Forgive and Forget?

You will remember that in an earlier chapter I drew a line between "not remembering," which I said was active and "forgetting," which I pointed out was passive. At that point I observed that God, the omnipotent Creator of the universe who knows all things, past, present, and future, does not forget. It is impossible for Him to do so (even though those who fail to observe the distinction between forgetting and not remembering often write as if God limited Himself in order to forget). Of course, that is not possible. God cannot deny His own nature. The problem is easily resolved by remembering that forgetting, a passive activity, belongs to human beings alone. But like God, they may also not remember.

Exactly what am I talking about in calling forgetting passive and not remembering active? By that I mean that one has direct control over not remembering but does not have control over forgetting. You can *not remember* in response to a command or a promise, but you have absolutely no control over forgetting. When you forget, it just happens. Remember that we said not remembering simply means not bringing a matter up to use it against another. When you promise to forgive another, you promise not to remember his wrongdoing by bringing it up to him, to others, or to yourself. That means you won't talk to others about it, and you won't allow yourself to sit and brood over it either.

The Bible never commands "forgive and forget." That is one of those old, unbiblical statements by which people often try to guide their lives that is utterly incorrect. If you try to forget, you will fail. In fact, the harder you try the more difficult you will find forgetting. That's because the more you attempt to do so, the harder you concentrate on the incident you are attempting (unsuccessfully) to forget.

The tale is told of the king whose exchequer was running low. So he called in all his alchemists and said, "Fellows, you've been working at this process of turning baser metals into gold for quite some time now. I need gold. This is Monday; I'll give you till Friday to come up with the formula or off go your heads." Friday came and heads rolled, one after another, until the king came to the last alchemist who said, "I've got it!"

The king replied, "You'd better, or your head will roll too. Let's hear the formula." So the alchemist told him: so much limestone, butterfly wings, a dash of lizard tongue— you name it! When he finished the king asked, "Is that it?"

"That's it," said the alchemist, and headed for the door.

"Don't leave town," said the king.

"Right," said the alchemist. But as he was leaving, he turned and said, "Oh, I forgot to tell you, King; if you think

of an elephant while you are stirring the pot, it won't work."
Needless to say, the alchemist died a natural death.

No, you just can't forget on command, and the Bible
doesn't require you to do so. It asks only that you model
your forgiveness after God's, and God promises to not remember.

No wonder Lewis Smedes sees forgiveness as a progressive program with several steps that must, in most cases,
take a long time and then only be partial. He believes that
one must forgive *and* forget, as the title of his book *Forgive
and Forget* clearly indicates.

*"Does that mean that I must go on thinking about that
horrible thing Joes did to me, again and again?"*

Absolutely not. You see, the wonderful thing about
God's forgiveness is this: When you make the promise to
not remember one's sins against him anymore and keep it,
you will find that *you will forget!* Indeed, the very best
way to forget is to keep the promise. If you don't rehearse
the wrongdoing to others or to yourself, more quickly than
you'd realize it will fade away. Forgiving is the only way
to forget.

Apologizing

*"In the very first chapter you referred to apologizing
as 'the world's substitute for forgiving.' What did you mean
by that?"*

Well, I meant exactly that. Whereas the Bible calls for
forgiveness, the world settles for apologizing. There is not
so much as a single reference to apologizing in the Bible.
It is a totally unscriptural concept.

"Where did it come from?"

No one knows the full history of apologizing, but the
name itself gives something of a clue. An apology is a
defense. An *apologia* was a defense made at a court trial
in ancient Greece. So, rather than admit wrong, apologizing originally was defending oneself against a charge of

doing wrong which, of course, is exactly the opposite of what confession of sin and seeking of forgiveness is all about.

In time apologizing became a milder sort of thing where, typically, one says, "I'm sorry." But to say, "I'm sorry," and to say, "I sinned against God and you; will you forgive me?" are two very different things.

"I can see some difference, but can you sharpen it up a bit?"

Certainly. Think about what happens in each transaction. When apologizing someone says, "I'm sorry." What has he done? Literally, all he has done is tell you how he feels. He *has not asked you to do anything.* When someone says, "I sinned; will you forgive me?" he is *asking you to make a promise to bury the matter once and for all.* In apologizing no commitment is made, the matter is not resolved, and the one who was wronged is not required to put the matter to rest. He is probably glad for the fact because in apologizing the wrongdoer has not even admitted his wrong. He has simply said he feels sorry about what happened. The principal difference between the two is simply this: God requires a commitment on the part of both parties that brings the matter to a satisfactory end. The world requires no such thing.

Picture the wrongdoer holding a basketball. He apologizes, saying, "I'm sorry." The one offended shuffles his feet awkwardly. It is always awkward to respond to an apology, because you are not asked to do anything, and yet some sort of response is expected. The offended party says something inane like, "Well, that's OK." But it isn't. The matter has not been put to rest. When you say the wrongdoing is OK you either lie or condone a wrong. At the end of the transaction the wrongdoer is still holding the ball.

Now, consider forgiveness. The wrongdoer comes with his basketball. He says, "I wronged you. Will you forgive me?" In so doing, he tosses the ball to the other person.

He is freed of his burden. Now, the burden for a response has shifted. The one wronged is asked to do what God requires him to do. He must either make the promise or risk offending God. There may be indecision on his part, but there is no awkwardness occasioned by unclarity. He knows what the Bible expects of him. When he says, "I forgive you," he promises not to bring the matter up again. The two have both made commitments. The wrongdoer confessed to wrongdoing; he committed himself to that confession. The offended party committed himself to burying the matter. At the end of the transaction, the ball is tossed away and obligations concerning the matter are over and done with. Both are free to become reconciled. The matter has been set to rest.

So, whenever you read in Christian books about apologizing (and you will, I can tell you) or hear Christians using this unbiblical substitute, make a correction in your mind. Say to yourself, "No. Apologizing doesn't do the trick. It is the world's unsatisfactory substitute that leaves the wrongdoer holding the ball." If it is practical, explain to those involved what the difference is. You can always blame your intrusion on me. You can say, "I was reading a book lately in which the writer distinguished between apologizing and forgiving. You see, he used this silly illustration concerning a basketball...."

Forgive God?

You may have a hard time believing it, but there are Christians who advise others to "forgive God." For instance, one writer says:

> Then I gently said, "Can you see what you have been doing to your husband and children? They cannot change [their height], and you have been angry toward them and God." I led her into a

prayer saying, "God, I ask forgiveness for my resentment and self-will. I forgive you for my husband and my sons being so short. And I thank You for them just the way they are."[21]

Can you believe it? First, the prayer is a contradiction in itself—thanking God that things are as they are and at the same time forgiving Him for having done the wrong thing in making those very same things that way. I'll leave it to you to sort that one out. Worse still is the idea that God needs to be forgiven. Tapscott is not alone in her belief. Helen Shoemaker writes: "Finally, there are those of us who need to forgive God."[22] God never does wrong. He is the very standard of right and wrong. By definition whatever He says or does is right because by nature He is absolutely holy. How can anyone purporting to be a Christian advise another to forgive God? The very idea borders on blasphemy and, at best, certainly is absurd.

Forgiving Self?

Ever since the modern emphasis on self flooded the church, along with the principles of the self-esteem movement, there has been an emphasis on forgiving oneself. Just as it is said that one has difficulty in loving himself, it is also said that he will have difficulty in forgiving himself. Listen to a few contemporary authors who make this claim.

Tapscott begins a six-page discussion of the subject by saying,

> It is so imperative that we accept God's forgiveness and forgive ourselves....Not forgiving ourselves is actually a form of rebellion....Do you suppose we are sinning when we do not forgive ourselves? This very act separates us from God. God's Word says we must forgive—that means even ourselves.[23]

[61]

Minirth and Meier likewise teach, "We need to forgive ourselves. Just as we get angry with other people, we become angry with ourselves...."[24]

Ron Lee Davis devotes an entire chapter to the subject and even claims that "the attempt [a mother] made against her baby's life was really an attempt to punish *herself,* by destroying her most precious and cherished possession....She was finally able to forgive herself."[25]

William Justice says, "The reconciled man has not only accepted forgiveness from God, but he has also forgiven himself."[26]

And, in a disappointing article by a theologian with whom I scarcely ever have reason to differ (or dare to), J.I. Packer, falling in line with the self-image teachers of today, writes:

> However unloved and worthless we once felt, and however much self-hate and condemnation we once nursed, we must now see that by loving us enough to redeem us God gave us value, and by forgiving us completely he obligated us to forgive ourselves and made it sin for us not to.[27]

And Smedes extols self-forgiveness in heroic language. "To forgive yourself takes high courage."[28]

Well, what of all this? Packer says that God made it sin for us not to forgive ourselves, and Tapscott agrees. Sin is failure to obey a command of God, whether by not doing what He requires or by doing what He forbids. Yet nowhere in the Bible are we commanded to forgive ourselves. It is a chancy thing, then, to extrapolate a command to forgive ourselves from the fact that God forgives us. This becomes especially doubtful when one couples this idea with the equally unbiblical idea that men have low self-esteem and, therefore, are commanded to love themselves. As is clear in the passages in which Jesus sums up the two commandments on love, He says, "On these *two* commandments hang all the law and the prophets." There is not a third commandment, and to represent the Bible as commanding love of self is therefore perilous. It risks putting commands in God's mouth. Just the same is true about forgiving self.

Both of these concepts, as Packer has seen, stand or fall together; they are of a piece. The problem supposedly is that men look down on themselves. But Jesus told us to love our neighbors *as ourselves*, implying that we already do pretty well in that regard and need instead to start working on loving our neighbor with some of the same devotion and concern that we already show ourselves. There is never, in all of the Word of God, a statement to the effect that men have a low self-image, that they must learn to love themselves, or that they must learn to forgive themselves. On the contrary, it is assumed that we do this without the slightest difficulty.[29]

So the Bible aims all its commands at turning our concern from self to God and others. It is not simply a matter of the Bible not using the jargon of the self-image teachers, as Packer thinks, but rather, a matter of the entire Bible knowing nothing of self-love, self-forgiveness concepts, and a doctrine of man that depicts him thinking so lowly of himself. It is not enough to *assert* that the Scriptures teach that man has a low self-image problem and, therefore, *command* him to think more highly of himself and learn to forgive himself. If we are told that not to do so is *sin*, biblical warrant for that fact must be clearly *demonstrated*. Otherwise, we have theologians, psychologists, and other writers placing new burdens on men's backs that they need not bear.

"But what is the problem then? Surely there are people who will tell you that they are having a hard time forgiving themselves. Haven't you ever had counselees who have said as much?"

[63]

Certainly, but their speech was filled with the lingo of the psychologists and others who propagate such things. I tell them, "You will never solve your problem by misunderstanding it as a problem of self-forgiveness."

"What do you tell them to do, then?"

Well, something like this. Suppose someone, through carelessness, runs over a child in his automobile and comes in saying, "Ill never be able to forgive myself for what I did." Or suppose a woman confesses the abortions she has had were murder and says much the same. I make it clear to them that the problem is not self-forgiveness. Their expressed agony stems from the very fact that, in the worst way, they *want* to forgive themselves. They want to put it behind them, they want to bury it once and for all. They want the burden of guilt lifted from their shoulders. If they had such low self-esteem as some think, they would instead be saying such things as, "Well, you'd expect someone like me to do that, wouldn't you?" Or, "I guess this is just true to form for a lout like me." But they don't. They say, "I don't know if I'll ever be able to forgive myself for what I've done," indicating they are certainly anxious to do so. Lack of ability to forgive self is not the problem.

The problem is that people who talk this way recognize something more needs to be done. Forgiveness is just the beginning; it clears away the guilt. They also recognize that they are still the same persons who did the wrong—that though they are forgiven, they have not changed. Without being able to articulate it, and using instead the jargon they have heard all around them, they are crying out for the change that will assure them they will never do anything like it again. When, as a counselor, I help them to deal with the problems in their lives that led to the wrong, in such a way that they have adopted a more biblical lifestyle, I then ask, "Are you still having trouble forgiving yourself?" Invariably, they say no.

[64]

What About the Unforgivable Sin?

In Matthew 12:22-33 we read:

Then a blind and dumb demoniac was brought to Him and He healed him, so that the dumb man spoke and saw. And all of the crowds were astonished and said, "Could He be David's Son?" But when the Pharisees heard this they said, "He can cast out demons only by Beelzebub, the ruler of demons."

Now because He knew their thoughts He said to them, "Every empire that is divided against itself comes to ruin, and every city or household that is divided against itself won't stand. So if Satan is casting out Satan, he is divided against himself. How then will his empire stand? And if I cast out demons by Beelzebub, by whom do your sons cast them out? Therefore they will be your judges. But if I cast out demons by God's Spirit, then God's empire has come upon you.

"Or, let Me ask you, how can anyone enter a strong man's house and steal his possessions unless he first binds the strong man? Then he can rob his house. Whoever isn't with Me is against Me, and whoever doesn't gather with Me scatters. So then I tell you all sorts of sins and blasphemies will be forgiven people, but the blasphemy against the Spirit will not be forgiven. And whoever speaks a word against the Son of Man will be forgiven, but whoever speaks against the Holy Spirit won't be forgiven, either in this age or in the coming one. Either consider the tree fine and its fruit fine, or consider the tree rotten and its fruit rotten, for trees are known by their fruit."

People become confused about the "unforgivable sin," thinking it to be masturbation, adultery, divorce, murder, not accepting Christ, etc. In the context it is none of these. The hardened, religious leaders of Judaism who wanted to reject Jesus and His teaching, which exposed their greed and hypocrisy, were looking for some way to "get Him." So they charged Him with casting out demons by the power of Beelzebub, the ruler of demons. They claimed He was in league with Satan. Actually, He was casting out demons by the power of the Holy Spirit (v. 28). In attributing the works of the Holy Spirit to an unclean spirit, they had blasphemed the *Holy* Spirit. This sin evidenced the very epitome of hardness to the truth of God. Persons who commit the unpardonable sin are: (1) not Christians and (2) are never concerned about becoming Christians. They are persons who are opposed to Jesus Christ and think that what He stands for is the work of the devil.

"That seems clear, but what about 1 John 5:16, where John tells us not to pray for the one who has committed a sin unto death?"

The verse ought to be translated this way:

If anybody sees his brother committing a sin that doesn't lead to death, he shall pray for him and He will give life to him (that is to those committing a sin that doesn't lead to death). There is a sin that leads to death; I don't say that you should ask questions about that.

Two distinct words are used. The first means "to ask for" something or "pray for" someone. The second means "to ask about" or "inquire about." John is not saying that the Christian must determine whether a brother has committed a sin that leads to death (see 1 Cor. 11:30) or not before he prays that God will give him life (presumably to

raise him from a sickbed). It is proper to pray for his healing at all times; don't trouble yourself to try to find out all
the details. Don't try to second-guess God. Just go ahead
and pray in all cases.

It seems that a new error is always turning up in the
discussion of forgiveness. But the fundamental issues have
been thought out for years. There are few advances to be
made in this area. New application of old truth, perhaps,
but rarely a new insight. Beware of those who claim to set
forth new truths or obligations regarding forgiveness.

7 *FORGIVENESS ISN'T ALL*

"**A** brother offended is harder to be won than a strong city, and quarrels are as bars of a castle." (Prov. 18:19)

"If he listens to you, you have won your brother." (Matt. 18:15)

"Go first and be reconciled to your brother." (Matt. 5:24)

"Forgive and comfort him, so that he won't be overwhelmed by too much pain. Therefore, I urge you to reaffirm your love to him." (2 Cor. 2:7-8)

In all these passages, one thing is uppermost—a concern for reconciliation.

Forgiveness is not an end in itself; it is a means to an end—a new and better relationship with those from whom we have become estranged because of some altercation. Not only does God want forgiveness to occur speedily, but His main interest is in the new relationship which forgiveness always ought to introduce. Forgiveness is clearing the rubble of the past so that something fresh and fine may be built in its place. Again, the divine model predominates, setting the pattern for us. In salvation, God does not merely forgive you, removing the guilt of your sin and promising never to bring up your wrongdoings, only to forget you thereafter. No. He goes on to establish a new relationship with you in which He wants you to grow close to Him. Too often "forgive and forget" means to forgive somebody—then forget him!

Because you can see that there must also be a positive side complementing forgiveness (which is essentially a negative thing: pulling the weeds before planting), it should also be apparent that a number of the errors we have had to confront virtually make such reconciliation impossible. Take for instance, the idea of unconditional forgiveness. J.M. Brandsma goes so far as to assert that "ignoring" a sin against one "...may include forgiveness."[30] This view strikes at the very core of forgiveness not only by eliminating the need to make the promise not to remember but also by removing the *inter*personal dimension. If Brandsma is correct, the person wronged need not confront or make a commitment, the offender need not repent, and neither party is obligated to work on building a new relationship. The same is true with the advice by David Augsburger and others not to tell a spouse about an affair. Such silence in the face of marital disruption provides no basis for repairing the relationship or working on problems that may have caused the disruption in the first place. No, the very idea of reconciliation as the goal of forgiveness precludes the forgiveness-as-unconditional doctrine.

So, reconciliation is the bigger picture of which forgiveness is only the initial element. This double dynamic of forgiveness and rebuilding is evident in Jesus' forgiveness and restoration of Peter. Peter denied the Lord around a charcoal fire after having boasted that if all the rest of the disciples denied Him, Peter would not. In the post-Resurrection account recorded in John 21:4-19, you can see how,

by referring to every aspect of the threefold betrayal, Jesus graciously enabled Peter to confess his sin in a thorough manner, and made it clear that all had been dealt with in its entirety. There was another charcoal fire (v. 9). Three times Peter is led to reflect on his lack of love, and the proud boast is handled directly in verse 15. But Jesus also made it possible for Peter to reassert his love for the Lord. Three times Jesus restored Peter to fellowship and reinstated him into his ministry. Beginning that day, Jesus was thereafter involved in building a new and more vital relationship with Peter. Reconciliation is essential.

Perhaps the best way to visualize this truth is by a diagram something like the following:

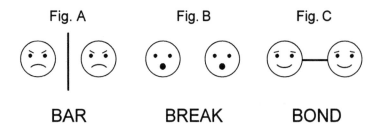

Fig. A   Fig. B   Fig. C

BAR   BREAK   BOND

In Figure A two persons are estranged; unforgiven sin, like a bar, separates them. In figure B forgiveness has taken place, and the bar has been removed. But that is not enough; there is still a break between them. In figure C through positive efforts toward reconciliation, a new bond has been established. For the process of reconciliation to occur, it must move through all three steps—from the removal of a bar to the establishment of a bond.

When matters are left at stage B, where wrong has been put off by forgiveness but no new relationship has begun, one can expect that other, usually worse, problems will arise between the parties involved. This principal Jesus affirmed in His story of the house swept clean, but left unoccupied

(Luke 11:24-26). In the biblical dynamic, the put-off must always be followed by the put-on. God's ways are never only negative when dealing with His people; He always follows the negative with a larger positive (see Rom. 5:20).

How about Help?

Often, in the early stages of the restoration of a relationship, outside help is necessary. Because I have written a number of books on help by biblical counseling, I shall not discuss how that help may best be given here. I shall simply indicate that if initial attempts at the restoration of a new and better relationship seem to fail (or seem likely to) because those involved do not know what to do, it is wise to bring in a third party. For those who want further details regarding the rebuilding of a relationship on new, more biblical lines, see my book *Ready to Restore* (Presbyterian and Reformed Pub. Co.).

The danger is to drift further apart. This can occur by doing nothing, or giving up when initial attempts at rebuilding seem unfruitful. You must not allow this to happen. At the earliest sign of failure, call for the help of a knowledgeable Christian brother or sister or your pastor. If not quickly followed by successful rebuilding activities, the awkwardness of confession and forgiveness is likely to create a polite coldness between the parties who, if nothing is done to counter it, will soon drift into a sterile relationship.

In 2 Corinthians 2:7-8, quoted at the head of this chapter, notice that Paul said three things were necessary to fully restore the repentant brother who had previously been put out of the church. In every case of reconciliation each of these is necessary to some extent. They are forgiveness, help, and reaffirmation of love.

Forgiveness, the subject of this book, needs no further discussion, but I must say a word about the other two. The second activity is translated "comfort." That is a correct translation but may, perhaps, be too specific here. The word

is a broad one that can refer to any sort of assistance or help needed. Assistance is the point to be emphasized when it is used in the context of reconciliation. A sinning brother or sister may easily become involved in all sorts of other sins while rebelling against God. Help of various sorts (financial, medical, etc.) may be required. In a reconciliation context, the wronged brother or sister may find it necessary to do far more for the forgiven offender than merely forgive him. He may not have the personal resources to provide such help, but he must, at least, pray for them, point the other party to the resources of the deacons of the church, or do whatever he can do to meet the need.

Efforts are not confined to one party alone. For instance, an adulterous spouse ought surely to have a thorough medical examination before recommencing sexual relations. This is the loving, kind thing to do. Otherwise, who knows what sorts of diseases he or she may bring into the marriage that may affect not only the spouse, but even future unborn children.

The very fact of looking for needs to meet in reestablishing a relationship, and then doing something about them is a factor that, when properly done, goes a long way toward reconciliation. People don't awkwardly drift apart when they are actively seeking to do good for one another. Contrary to what many think today, relationships are not built out of the blue. You can't just "work on a relationship" in the abstract. Relationships grow out of common concerns, joint activities, and going through difficulties together. They grow from problems unitedly faced and overcome in a biblical way. They grow incidentally, as a byproduct. They are never built directly. The concern shown for the repentant person (and by him) must be genuine. It must be done for his benefit in order to please God.

Reaffirm Love

The third factor mentioned in 2 Corinthians 2:8 is to reaffirm love. The word reaffirm is a specialized term, used only here in the New Testament, meaning to officially reinstate. When one repents and is readmitted into the church, he may not be accepted as a second-class citizen of the kingdom of God. God has no such citizens. The repentant one comes back with full rights and privileges of membership in the church. He is not barred from singing in the choir for six months and so forth. Now in most reconciliation contexts, someone will not be reentering the church after having been disciplined out of it, but, in an *unofficial* way, the same thing holds. Neither you nor others should remain aloof from the brother or sister who is reinstated. Full fellowship must be restored. He should be restored with active, loving words and deeds by all. You can set the example. If you see others hesitating, you can make efforts to include them as well. If some are inclined to give the repentant brother the cold shoulder, it may even be necessary to speak directly to them about this, pointing out that in doing so, they are resisting the commands of this passage.

Clearly, then, restoration is not something that may be taken lightly or done casually. One must consciously work at it. It will take time, creativity, energy, perhaps even money. But it is so important that, apart from this positive side of the watershed, the forgiveness on the other side may be worthless.

While restoration is essential to fellowship, it need not always be to a level of deep friendship. Jesus called all His disciples "friends" (John 15:13-15), but, of these, three seemed closest. These He took onto the Mount and into the Garden. And of these three, one was the closest: the disciple whom Jesus "loved."

This chapter is brief, but it is important. If you don't know where to begin, perhaps you ought to sit down with the one with whom you desire to be reconciled, read this chapter together (one reason I wanted to keep it short), and discuss what must be done positively to establish a new and better relationship between you.

8 WHAT ABOUT UNBELIEVERS?

കൈ്ൈകൈ്ൈകൈ്ൈകൈ്ൈകൈ്ൈകൈ്ൈകൈ്ൈകൈ്ൈകൈ്ൈകൈ്ൈ

A dmittedly, there are problems concerning biblical forgiveness and non-Christians. There are severe limitations on what can be achieved.

In Romans 12:18, we read some of the most important words ever penned concerning the relationship of believers to unbelievers. "If possible, so far as it depends on you, be at peace with all men." The phrase "all men" includes unbelievers.

What makes this verse so important is the way in which the command is qualified. The first qualification recognizes the fact that when dealing with unbelievers, results may be less than satisfactory. That is why Paul says, "If possible." Those words strike a note of stark realism. In our relationships with unbelievers, our expectations must be realistic. Unbelievers do not know the true God, they are self-centered rather than oriented toward God and others, they do not possess the Holy Spirit, and so cannot love God or man in ways that are acceptable to God (Rom. 8:5; 1 Cor. 2). They cannot understand the Bible (1 Cor. 2:6-16), and if they did, they wouldn't want to follow it, or couldn't. In short, as Paul put it, "Those who are in the flesh [unbelievers] *cannot* please God" (Rom. 8:8).

It is a most realistic statement indeed. It is, at once, a disturbing and a freeing qualification. Disturbing, in that expectations are so low; freeing, in that it exempts believers from the discouraging task of attempting the impossible.

Notice that there is a second qualification as well: "So far as it depends on you." These words indicate that the only one who can be expected to act properly in such a relationship is the believer. Every proper relationship demands at least two parties working at it. From the believer's side, everything must be done to preserve peace. But, at best, even the sort of peace anticipated here is not the full-orbed *shalom,* with all its blessings and benefits, that Jesus gives His people (John 14:27). It is the mere cessation of hostilities.

The believer, relying on the Word and the Spirit, can go a long way toward establishing and maintaining peace by obedience to Scripture. If he follows to the full the principles of forgiveness and reconciliation outlined here, at least half of the relationship will be developed in a biblical manner. And, of course, his words, attitudes, and actions will be pleasing to the Lord. Frequently this brings peace.

Can an Unbeliever Repent?

Suppose John, a Christian is cheated by Milton, an unbeliever, in a business deal. Now that the work has been completed, Milton claims that he quoted a price of $500 for a painting job, and John knows that he said, "No more than $350." In a kind and respectful way, John will have to point out the truth. If John cannot afford to stand the loss, and Milton will not relent, John may have to take the matter to small claims court. He doesn't have a written estimate, but he does have a witness—a neighbor who heard Milton's original quotation. Suppose, however, when confronted with the neighbor and the threat to take him to court, Milton says, "I'm sorry, I needed the money badly, and I thought I could make a little more that way." He *apolo-*

gizes. We have seen that apologizing creates an awkward situation in which matters are never set to rest. What should John do?

May he grant Milton forgiveness? Well, let's consider matters as closely as we can. Under pressure, Milton confessed his sin. He is sorry he was caught. He will back down. But his "repentance" is not sorrow over having offended a holy God. Milton isn't saying, "Lord, I have sinned against You." He may not even be sorry that he attempted to rob you. (He may have justified this to himself out of self-pity.) He regrets his lying and attempted theft for selfish reasons. He thinks, "My reputation may suffer and I will lose jobs. It is embarrassing to have to admit to my wrongdoing," and so on. That is very different from biblical repentance. So, in no sense does Milton's confession fall within the parameters of Luke 17. The difference is between the two sorts of repentance mentioned by Paul in 2 Corinthians 7. Acceptable repentance, as Paul says, is the result of sorrow that comes from God and is a repentance that no one need regret (2 Cor. 7:10). But, further on in the same verse he also mentions sorrow that comes from the world, leading to a "repentance" unacceptable to God, and ending in death (v. 10).

So, there are two kinds of repentance stemming from two distinct sources: God and the world. One we might call true repentance—a desire to change because of regret over sin against God. The other is a bogus repentance, occasioned by regret about personal loss or inconvenience. The two are as distinct as their sources.

So then, can an unbeliever repent? No. If he truly repented, he would by definition be a believer. Surely you have noticed already that the verses concerning forgiveness, with which we have been dealing, appear in a context of brotherly relationships. They do not have to do with the relationship of a believer to an unbeliever. Frequently, the word "brother" actually occurs, clearly indicating that what is being taught pertains to the sphere of family relationships in the household of God.

Milton and John

Well, then, what does John do when Milton confesses? He thanks him for telling the truth and for adjusting the bill. If he has known about this matter prior to the confrontation, he has prayed for Milton and for himself: that Milton may come to know Christ somehow through this experience and that John may honor Christ in it. He has also, when praying, forgiven in his heart—that is, as we have seen previously, he has told God of his willingness to forgive and has asked God to free him from all bitterness and resentment. That's the first thing he must do.

Now, in pursuing peace with all men, and in doing all he can from his side of the relationship to procure peace, John will try to use this opportunity to win Milton to Christ. Or, if that does not seem appropriate at the moment, he may ask God that this encounter may become a foundation from which he may do so in the future. John knows that real peace can come only through peace with God.

One way to present Christ to Milton might be through this very issue we have been discussing. After Milton confesses, John may say something like this to Milton:

I am sorry you're having hard times, and I will surely pray that God will enable you to meet your expenses in an honest way. If I get a little extra money, I'll try to help. You know, Milt, I really wish I could forgive you for what you have done, but I can't. I've forgiven you in my heart, and I'll hold no grudges, but I can't make the promise that I'll never bring this matter up again. In fact, I'd like to keep it open long enough to tell you how in Christ you can get God Himself to forgive not only this, but all your sins. You see....

Of course, this is but the bare bones of one possible approach. Approaches and responses to each circumstance will vary. But what better context would there be for presenting the Gospel than one in which you are discussing the forgiveness of sins? It may be that in a more relaxed setting, sometime later, when John is chatting with Milt after a round of golf, he may want to raise the issue. But be careful not to rationalize here. Often a situation like this, in spite of its ragged edges, offers the best opportunity for witnessing. In times like these people tend to think more seriously about their lives. While he may storm off in a huff or brush your attempt aside, Milton cannot help but think about what you say. God often uses such situations to plant the seed that He will germinate later on.

Turn the Tables, Will You?

"Christians aren't sinless. Suppose, for a moment, I am the one at fault and I must go and confess my sins to some unbeliever I have wronged. How does that work?"

Let's suggest another scenario. Your name is Sally, and you are a Christian. You belong to the local garden club, which is a mixed bag of believers and unbelievers. At a meeting of the nominating committee, of which you are a part, you fear that your recommendation of a fine, Christian member will be turned down by the others on the committee in favor of an unbelieving woman you are sure will make life miserable for everyone during the coming year. In the discussion of the second potential nominee, you refer to something you know she did, but you use a good deal of license in presenting the "facts." As a result, her nomination fails. At home that night you discuss the matter with your husband, and he has the courage to gently point out your sin and ask what you are going to do about it.

What should you do? Well, to begin with, you need to get on that phone and call every member of the nominating committee and ask them to meet with you as soon as possible—before announcing the nominee. The gracious thing to do is to invite them to lunch at your home. Then, amidst their puzzlement, you must confess:

> What I said about Patty the other day wasn't altogether true. Because I was afraid she would be nominated, and I didn't think she'd make a good president, I embellished the truth. It is not true that she did so and so or that she said thus and thus. Please forgive me for lying to you and influencing your vote by information that is untrue. I still think she'd be wrong for president, but I sinned against her, against you, and, most of all, against God. That is why I called this meeting. Though I certainly didn't act like one when I was with you the other day, I am a Christian. And as a Christian I have failed God and the rest of you. Please forgive me for leading you astray. You may wish to reconsider your vote in the light of the truth.

Then, since gossip is so prevalent, and Patty has by now heard (or will soon hear) the falsehoods you told about her, you should go to Patty and ask her forgiveness as well. But go after straightening things out with the nominating committee. You will want to tell Patty not only about your lies but also about how you rectified the situation.

You may wonder, *Can an unbeliever forgive?* The answer is no. That's why the apology system was developed in the place of genuine, biblical forgiveness. Because he knows nothing of God's forgiveness, he certainly can't imitate it. Nor can his heart be right if he attempts to do so (he makes no promise before God; he doesn't have the power of God to enable him to keep a promise; his motives are all wrong). But, nevertheless, you must ask him to forgive you. You must do the right thing, and he is required to do so too. God Himself regularly commands unbelievers to do what is right, even when He knows they can't. Ability is not the measure of responsibility. Again, in explain-

ing something of forgiveness, you may find (or make) an opening for the Gospel.

Cats and Dogs

Cats meow and dogs bark. You don't expect to hear a dog meow or a cat bark. Each animal acts according to its nature. It should be no surprise to you when unbelievers act like unbelievers. That also should be expected. They act according to their natures. So too should believers act according to the new nature with which they are being renewed. Yet, at times, they don't. But it should come as no surprise when believers sin. In fact, the whole elaborate system of forgiveness about which you have been thinking as you study this book makes it abundantly clear that God expected Christians to sin. Otherwise, there would have been no need for Him to establish the processes of church discipline and forgiveness. That cats meow and dogs bark is essentially what Paul is saying. Perhaps, more accurately put: cats meow and dogs *should* bark. (You can turn that around if you prefer cats to dogs as I do!)

Because the unbeliever is not subject to Christ or His church it is impossible to use the formal aspects of church discipline in dealing with him. However, it is never wrong to follow at least the first two steps of informal discipline mentioned in Matthew 18:15-16. Under these directions you may confront the unbeliever about his sin and at least attempt to work matters out the best way possible. If that fails, it certainly would be wise to call in a third party to attempt to bring about a solution. If that fails, and he refuses to hear you, there is every indication that you may (if appropriate, and you wish to do so) take him to court to obtain justice.

Though 1 Corinthians 6 forbids Christians taking other *Christians* to court, and insists that you should work matters out within the framework of the church itself as a family matter, it does allow you to take unbelievers before unbelieving judges. In other words, at the point in the process of discipline where one would "tell it to the church," instead, one may "tell it to the court." Just as there is a two-step process in telling it to the church (first to the elders and then to the whole body), so there is a two-step process in taking one to law. As confrontation by the elders may be all that is necessary to bring about repentance on the part of the believer, so confrontation by your lawyer may be all that is necessary to obtain results from an unbeliever. In neither case may full process be necessary. Court cases are a battle, and if there is any biblically legitimate way to avoid them, you should.

There are three persons in every relationship: The other person, you, and God. You are not in this alone. God is there, observing, and at work. He is concerned to see that you do the right thing at each point, attempting to be a peacemaker if at all possible. You can count on Him always to do the right thing in relationship to both of you. Scripture refers to God's part in the relationship when it says, "When a man's ways please the Lord, He makes even his enemies to be at peace with him" (Prov. 16:7).

So what is the upshot of this chapter? Simply this: you do not have as many resources in dealing with an unbeliever as you do in a relationship with a Christian, so you must not expect the same results. One thing you can always do is to please God in your relationship to the unbeliever by making sure that there is nothing left undone on your side of the relationship. If there is not peace, you must be certain that that is entirely because of the unwillingness of the unbeliever to have it, never because of some fault of yours.

9 KEEPING THE PROMISE

Surely Lewis Chafer was wrong when he penned, "Forgiveness on the part of one person toward an other is the simplest of duties."[31]

We have seen already that the duty of forgiveness requires one to take unpleasant actions that I've referred to as rheumatism and gout, and to think through complex theoretical issues that have not always been handled well. Now we must consider the practical matter of keeping the promise you made when you granted another forgiveness.

As you now know, when you forgive another, you declare that you are canceling his debt, removing his guilt, and promising that you will never again bring up his guilt, and promising that you will never again bring up his offenses to use against him. The promise involved three things.

1. I will not bring the matter up to you.
2. I will not bring the matter up to another.
3. I will not bring the matter up to myself.

How about Consequences?

Freddy's parents have forgiven him for his reckless driving which endangered the lives of other drivers and pedestrians. Freddy has repented. There was no accident and no one was injured, but Freddy received a ticket with a whopping fine that he is working hard to pay off. The matter is closed.

At the time of forgiveness, however, there was some discussion that may be of interest to you. Freddy maintained that since his guilt had been removed and his debt canceled, Dad ought to pay the fine. Otherwise, Dad was holding his sin against him. Is that true? Was Freddy right?

Of course not. Mom and Dad had forgiven his sin and would have to be careful not to harp on his past driving record, even though they might feel like doing so. But in forgiving him they did not promise to remove all the *consequences* of the offense.

When David sinned against God by adultery and murder, God forgave him (Ps. 51 is a firm record of that fact), but He did not remove all the consequences. David's child died. When a profligate sinner turns to Christ, he does not sprout a new arm in the place of the one that he lost in a drunken brawl when he shoved it through a plate-glass window. When Bill forgives Tom for stealing his lawnmower, he is not wrong in asking for its return. Repentance demands restitution in those cases in which it can be made.

Some consequences, however, are more subtle. If not handled properly, working out their implications may even border on breaking the threefold promise of forgiveness. It is important, therefore, to distinguish very carefully those things that differ.

Take, for example, counseling or other help aimed at fortifying a person against future transgressions. Obviously in such efforts a counselor will explore the past to discover patterns that must be guarded against if one is to grow strong

enough to resist future transgressions. That means the sin, and possibly others similar to it, will have to be brought up. This time when sins are brought up it must be done in an *entirely* helpful way with no bitterness, or vindictiveness. In other words, it is important to distinguish between bringing up a sin in order to help someone and bringing it up to use it against him.

Sometimes, people fail to draw these lines sharply enough. If you are helping another, it is most important to err on the side of caution. Picture a husband and wife in whose marriage there has been a great deal of bickering. Each has forgiven the other, especially for the last episode which was so intense it drove them to counseling. Now they are working with their pastor who is trying to discover what sorts of things they quarrel over, how quarrels begin, and so forth. In this way he can help them structure their relationship against future altercations. But unless the pastor is very careful to mention the danger of possible infractions of their promises, it will be very easy for the couple to cross the line into forbidden territory when describing the past.

What makes the problem so subtle and, therefore, difficult to deal with, is the fact that the very same sentences may be spoken helpfully or hurtfully. The manner in which the words were spoken, the purpose for saying them, and the attitude underlying them makes all the difference. Since the heart belongs to God, and you cannot judge motives, you can do but two things to offset the problem. First, you must warn against it plainly and persistently. Second, you must take a person's word for it when he says there was no bitterness or vindictiveness in what he said. In love, until the facts prove otherwise, you must "believe all things, hope all things" (1 Cor. 13:7). That means you must give everyone the benefit of the doubt.

What Happens When You Break the Promise?

Let's say you get exasperated at someone who has "done it again," for the umpteenth time, and burst out, "You'll never change. There you go again! Why that's the tenth time you've done that to me! It looks like you're never going to be any different. All your promises and all your regrets don't mean a thing. I've had it!"

Breaking your promise to forgive, you have thrown another's past sin into his teeth. That is sin on your part.

What should you have done? Well, you could have mentioned that the person involved seems to be having a hard time overcoming the problem, and you could have offered more than forgiveness this time. You could also offer to help him overcome the difficulty. If you haven't the faintest idea about how to help, you could encourage (*encourage*, not nag) him to see a pastor.

"OK, that's clear enough. But now, let's suppose I don't follow that procedure. Suppose I lose control and lash out in a manner similar to that which you have described. What do I do then?"

The first thing you must do is recognize that you have sinned in breaking your promise. Unless you see your act as sin, you will never become serious enough about it to change. Recognizing your words as sin, *you* must now seek forgiveness both from God and the offended party. Then perhaps the two of you should find the help you need to overcome each of your problems.

Often just the fact that the other party is working on his problem from a biblical perspective—learning to replace sinful patterns with righteous ones—makes all the difference. Any small signs of growth are encouraging. If it is agreeable for you to help in this growth process by reminding or checking up, that too, done out of loving concern, brings hope. These things take the pressure off and allow for the other person to err without the sky falling in. So, if

[85]

possible and desirable, try to offer personal help. Helping another often helps you as well by putting you on your mettle.

What if I Must Do It Alone?

Rarely do you ever have to grow in grace alone. Jesus Christ expects His people to help one another. Consider all those New Testament "one another" passages in which believers are exhorted to stimulate one another to love and good works, to comfort one another, to teach one another, and so on. If no one offers, you may have to request help. Others may be hesitant to approach you, may not realize you have a problem, or may not think you want help. When you need help, ask. If you don't, then don't blame anyone else.

But there may be rare occasions when you can't find anyone to help, or you may want to try to overcome the problem on your own. What then?

In order to overcome the problem of promise-breaking, try carrying a Philippians 4:8 think list. This can be especially helpful to those who are having trouble disciplining their minds. Paul tells us to focus our thinking on the things that fit the categories listed in Philippians 4:8:

Finally, brothers, whatever is true, whatever is serious, whatever is just, whatever is pure, whatever is lovely, whatever is of good repute, if there is anything morally excellent and if there is anything praiseworthy, think on these things.

If you find yourself dwelling on what someone did to you, you need help. Remember you promised not to bring up the matter—to *yourself.* That means all brooding, feeling sorry for yourself, and so on, is sin.

Mary had such a problem. She had forgiven her husband Pete for his adultery, but every day when he returned home, he'd find her either in tears or morose and red-eyed from crying. It was misery for him to live with. Pete had sincerely repented, had truly broken off the affair, and had been forgiven. *Why must she keep on brooding over it? It is a form of punishing me,* he thought.

When confronted by her pastor about it, Mary replied, "No, I don't want to punish Pete. I know, if anything, my weakness has provided occasion for further problems between us, but I just can't seem to help myself. When I sit there thinking about her in his arms...." She broke into sobs.

Mary's pastor said, "What are you doing thinking such things? You forgave Pete. That means you promised not to remember his sins against him anymore."

"I know, Pastor, but it's so hard. I'm sitting there and the thoughts just come. I don't plan to do it."

"But Mary, how have you planned not to do it?"

"What do you mean, Pastor?"

"Just that. If you want to overcome the problem, you must plan not to sin, structure against it, and follow your plan assiduously. In Romans 12:17 we read, 'Plan ahead to do what is fine in the eyes of everyone.'

"If you want to meet the enemy in battle, you don't improvise on the spot. Instead you drill for months until you know what to do. If you want to preach a sermon that is a blessing to others, you study long hours in preparation. To do anything well, you must plan ahead.

"Overcoming your problem takes prior planning. Fortunately it takes even less planning than preparing a dinner. I suggest you use a Philippians 4:8 think list."

"What is that, Pastor?"

"Simply a list of things to think about whenever you find your mind wandering toward areas into which it should not trespass. Here's what you should do. Take a piece of paper and write the numbers 1-20 on it. Next to each write out a carefully thought-out, mind-engaging topic to which

you need to give some thought. Don't list airy abstractions, such as the immensity of the universe, about which you can think for only a few seconds. Fill the page with practical matters such as, "What do I have to do to prepare for our vacation this summer?" That will probably not only engage your mind, but you will find yourself using pencil and paper before you are through. Here, I'll give you your first item on the list as a freebie. Write this down: 'Things to put on my list,' If you start thinking about that, you'll get the other 19.

"Now, whenever you catch your mind wandering, whip out your list, ask the Lord to help you keep your mind on those things that are profitable, and go to work. Carry your list with you wherever you go, making new lists as needed, until such a time as your mind begins to travel the proper paths on its own."

"I see. Do you think that it will work, Pastor?"

"Many other persons who have had similar problems have found that it does. But you have to be serious about it. You must really want to change. You can't enjoy even the slightest remnants of self-pity. You must ruthlessly discipline your mind—that means regularity and consistency.

"Now, there is one other factor I would like to mention, Mary. You talked about when you are 'sitting there the thoughts just come,' or something like that."

"That's right, Pastor. Every afternoon when I'm sitting in my chair waiting for Pete to come home, I find my mind wandering into that 'forbidden territory.'"

"Well, you must do something about that too. Probably you need to rearrange your schedule. And you need to omit periods in which you just aimlessly sit and think. During the next two months while you are working on the problem, never let yourself sit and think without planning ahead of time what you will think about. You need also to consider whether you have too much time on your hands when you are alone. Perhaps as you reexamine your daily schedule you will find that there is some time during the week when you can do some volunteer work at the church, visit some invalids in the congregation, or whatever. But at all costs you must not allow yourself long periods of idle time when you are doing nothing profitable."

Such practical measures are not only important, but in most cases they are absolutely necessary when beginning to discipline your thinking. If you are having problems keeping a promise to not bring a matter up to yourself (the place where most fail), you need to follow the Philippians 4:8 think list procedure, or develop some other equally effective program. But—and this is the most important consideration of all—whatever you do, *you must plan it ahead of time.*

No, forgiveness is not "the simplest of duties," but neither is it impossible. A practical, biblically derived approach will enable you to live a life much more honoring to Christ and more loving to your neighbor. Why didn't I say "and more satisfying to you"? Because I want to consider that question in the next chapter. Ask Jesus to help you get to work today; it is worth it.

10 FOR WHOSE SAKE?

ᖇᖇᖇᖇᖇᖇᖇᖇᖇᖇᖇᖇᖇᖇᖇᖇᖇᖇᖇᖇᖇᖇᖇᖇ

One theme runs through many of the current books that have to do with forgiveness. Perhaps it is best encapsulated in the title of Richard Walters' book, *Forgive and Be Free, Healing the Wounds of Past and Present.* The theme is that you should forgive others because it will do you good.

This self-orientation of modern forgiveness literature emerges not only in the unbiblical notion of an imagined duty to forgive oneself (see chapter six), but, more fundamentally, in a widespread misunderstanding of the purpose of forgiving.

I have already commented on David Augsburger's advice to a husband not to tell his wife about his sin in order to seek her forgiveness if he can "get relief" from confessing his sin to God alone. Here, the concern focuses solely on the husband; the wife is not considered. In his book *Forgive and Forget,* Smedes speaks of "our need to forgive *for our own sakes.* "[32] He continues, "When you forgive someone for hurting you, you perform spiritual surgery inside your soul."[33]

Walters assures his readers that "this book will illus-
trate how forgiving has changed people's lives and will
coach you in the process of forgiving so that you can attain
the full measure of joy available to you."[34]

And the reason that Betty Tapscott wants you to forgive animals, countries, and denominations (see chapter
three) is to set you free (the descriptive subtitle of her book).
Obviously, such self-deceptive pretenses at forgiveness
(when they think it through, everybody knows you cannot
really promise an animal, a country, or denomination anything) are strictly self-centered: to "get relief", as David
Augsburger puts it. The whole concern throughout the book
is for the one who did the wrong. Little or none is shown
for the one who was wronged.

On Whom Should Concern Be Focused?

When He forgave, what was Christ's concern? His
entire emphasis was on the honor of God and the blessing
of the one whose sins were forgiven (see such passages as
John 5:14; Mark 2:5, 12). Even when He makes it clear
that the Father will not hear your prayer for forgiveness
unless you forgive others, the way in which He puts it is
not so much an incentive to forgive but a warning that if
you don't, you will be in trouble with your Heavenly Father. Never does He even so much as suggest that the reason for forgiving another is to find personal relief. This
self-oriented motive for forgiveness is foreign to the Bible.

Yet, in our time, it is that very motive that is the interest
and concern of most who write about the forgiveness of
others. Why is that? Because of the wholesale takeover of
Christian thought and writing by psychology, from which
such notions come. Self-interest is everywhere manifested,
whether it be in forgiving self, seeking to develop a better
self-image, looking for security and significance for oneself, or, as here, doing something good for another in order
to obtain a benefit for oneself.

On the contrary, Jesus taught us to look away from self, to crucify self, deny self, and be concerned instead about God and others. He set forth two great commandments as the summary of all the Bible teaches: to love God and to love one's neighbor. There, He pointed away from self to others. In Philippians 2:3-4, Paul likewise stressed the same thing.

Is Granting Forgiveness Mere Bargaining?

From the way those who talk about the therapeutic results to one who forgives another, you would think they were selling snake oil. My guilt feelings, my headaches, my misery, etc., will be relieved if only I strike a bargain with God. He will take them away *if* I forgive others. Put the forgiveness coin in the slot, push the right buttons, and out will come the desired boon. God becomes a cosmic dispensing machine. No, God is a Person, and you must never forget it. Your transactions with Him are transactions of the heart, into which He looks and perceives your motives. If your motives are self-centered, your relationship with Him will go sour. You must not pray for another, or "when you stand praying," tell God that you will forgive another, when your purpose is to obtain such and such a boon in return.

Like God's, your forgiveness must be "gracious." In Ephesians 4:32, "Be kind, one to the other, tenderhearted, forgiving one another, just as God, for Christ's sake has forgiven you," the verb for forgiveness stresses the graciousness of the act of forgiveness. Not only is true forgiveness undeserved, but it is always granted out of mercy (kind tender-heartedness), certainly not for the ulterior purpose of obtaining something for oneself!

The word used is *charizomai*, a verbal form of the noun *charis*, "grace." It means "to give something to someone *freely*, as a favor." Every nuance in the word and in the verse focuses on the one who is forgiven. There is no expressed or implied interest in the one doing the forgiving (cf. Col. 3:13). His welfare in the act or what benefits might possibly accrue to him are never in view.

Well, are there benefits? Certainly, but like joy and peace, these are by-products, not to be sought (or found) as ends in themselves. An improvement in one's relationship with God and with the other person is one obvious benefit noted in the New Testament. But, the emphasis is not there. The emphasis is on what one may do to help another who has repented of his sin. As always, the New Testament stresses love—an other-oriented giving of oneself, possessions, time, interest, or whatever it is that the other needs. Biblical love, like God's, is not love with strings attached; it is love that thinks of the welfare of another while forgetting self. It is giving by forgiving. That is why I have spoken of "granting" forgiveness. It is giving *another* a freedom he does not deserve. Forgiveness is gracious. The appeal in the modern books, intentionally or otherwise, is to selfishness. That is a thoroughly unbiblical motivation.

What then is the purpose of granting others forgiveness? To do some good for yourself? No. It is to do good to another out of gratitude to God, honoring Him by emulating His gracious forgiveness in Christ.

Friend, think carefully about the spirit in which you forgive another. If you are still angry at him, at least go out of gratitude toward God, with whom you are not angry, and to whom you owe everything in Christ. Be sure you rid your heart of all self-seeking as you go. Otherwise, there will be no spirit of kindness and tenderheartedness in what you do. It is only when you stop thinking of your hurts and the injustice done to you, and turn instead to the great need of one who has done such a wrong and has now come to see the enormity of what he did, that you will forgive in kindness and tenderheartedness. Forgiveness must always move outward toward God (honoring Him through obedience out of gratitude) and the one to be forgiven (out of

concern for his welfare), rather than inward toward self (the benefits and boons which will be mine if I forgive another).

11 REPENTANCE, CONFESSION, & FORGIVENESS

পথঃপথঃপথঃপথঃপথঃপথঃপথঃপথঃপথঃপথঃপথঃপথঃ

Throughout discussions in this book, the two biblical words repentance and confession are freely used. I have set forth both repentance and confession as prerequisites for forgiveness. But to what does each refer? In this chapter, I want to help you understand the terms, what they refer to, and their relationship to forgiveness.

Repentance Is a Powerful Thing

What is the powerful thing called repentance that, if a man even *says* he has it, must be honored? (Luke 17:3) Is it a deep sorrow and grief, as some have thought? Is it an act of man or a work of God?

Surely sorrow may accompany repentance, but it must never be equated with it. Weeping does not necessarily connote true repentance (see Deut. 1:42ff). Unfortunately, the King James Version translated two distinct words "repentance," thereby confusing many. The word that should not have been so translated was the one that is inseparably connected with sorrowful feelings. It should instead be translated "regret." Repentance is not a feeling. A person

may regret his words or actions, as Esau did, but not be repentant. Regret comes from many causes and may be *mixed* with true repentance, but real repentance comes only from the honest acknowledgment of sin.

As there can be sorrow without repentance so can there be repentance that only later produces sorrow. Sorrow without repentance is a sorrow for oneself. Sorrow that accompanies repentance is a sorrow over one's sin against God and his neighbor.

The Old Testament word for repentance means literally, "to turn." It indicates an about-face in one's thinking that leads to an about-face in his lifestyle (thoughts and ways). In the New Testament, that same idea is continued. Jesus told Peter, "When you have been converted [literally, 'turned around'] strengthen your brethren" (Luke 22:32), but to this is added the kindred image of "rethinking, changing one's mind" (the dominant New Testament word). To repent, then, indicates a mental about-face or alteration of thought which leads to a change of life.

Perhaps this idea is most sharply set forth in Isaiah 55:7-8, "Let the wicked forsake his way, and the unrighteous man his schemings; let him return to the Lord, an He will have mercy on him, to our God, for He will abundantly pardon. For My thoughts are not your thoughts, neither are your ways My ways, says the Lord."

In calling Israel to repentance, God, through Isaiah, demands that she "forsake" her thoughts and ways, because they are not His ways—which He sets over against theirs. Instead, He insists she must begin thinking His thoughts after Him, and walking in His ways (v. 9). These "higher" thoughts and ways, God maintains, have been revealed in the Bible (vv. 10-11). In a word, then, repentance is turning from one's own sinful thoughts and ways to biblical truth and holiness.

A Change of Mind

About what must a Christian change his thinking in the repentance that is the condition for forgiveness? Surely the believer must abandon all thoughts that lead him to suppose he can get away with his sin. The very act of confrontation by another brother (Luke 17:3; Matt. 18:15) should make that clear. God wants sin exposed for what it is.

Moreover, if he has deceived himself into thinking his sin is a good that will bring him joy and benefit, he must recognize that this is a delusion. No one who is God's child can ever think for long that hurting another through his wrongdoing is a way to happiness or blessing. On the contrary, he must remember the Cross as the time of supreme grief brought about by wrongdoing.

If he had any thought of continuing his sinful behavior toward God and others, he must come to the place where he realizes that this is impossible, and that he must cease and desist. If his heart has become hardened to the breaking of his relationship to God and others so that he does not care, repentance is the rekindling of concern. All this is the work of the Holy Spirit applying His Word (often through the ministry of other believers).

In these, and any other ways in which a situation calls for a change of mind, repentance means such an alteration of one's thoughts, beliefs, and attitudes that he now sees his sins for what they really are. Repentance is a turning from self-aggrandizement to a humility that recognizes oneself as unworthy before God and man. Self-worth teaching today, brought into the church from pagan psychologies, tends to fortify persons against repentance. Such teachings must be resisted as detrimental to Christian repentance. Repentance is a change in one's outlook that lifts his eyes from self and his own affairs, enabling him to "seek first the kingdom of God and His righteousness" (Matt. 6:33).

Repentance is a prerequisite to forgiveness because until one rethinks his attitudes and actions, bringing them into conformity to God's so that he thinks like Him, there is no possibility for the change of lifestyle implied in the plea, "Forgive me." Neither reconciliation nor communion with God and neighbor is possible.

One can make the promise "not to remember" to another when he says, "I repent," because when he says so, he is understood as saying, "I have been wrong; I do not want to do this again." Repentance is the opposite of excuse-making and alibis. It is a frank admission of wrong thinking that led to wrongdoing. On hearing such an admission of sin, the forgiving person can ask for no more. He must lift the burden from his brother or sister's shoulders and free him to become his friend once more.

Confession of Sin

Confession is inseparably linked with repentance; it is the outward expression to others of the inner admission to oneself that one was wrong in thought, word, attitude, or deed. It is a verbal admission of wrongdoing made in the presence of the wronged party.

The word *confess* means literally, "to say the same thing." It is, therefore, verbal agreement to the scriptural evaluation of his behavior as sin. The word is used of contracts where two or more parties come to an "agreement." Here in a very real sense the wrongdoer is saying he is willing to sign a contract with God and his brother stating that he was wrong and that he seeks forgiveness. In a sense the entire forgiveness transaction is a contractual event with agreements, promises, and so forth. Of course, since the Bible requires no such thing, I am not for a moment suggesting that an actual, written contract be drawn up. It is, however, as solemn an event as if one were signing his name to a contract, when he confesses his sin to another *in the presence of God*. And it is every bit as solemn an act to make the promise of forgiveness.

Confession is saying to another, "You are right. I did wrong you; I did sin against you." It is admitting what has been charged, or, as in some cases some part of what has been charged, as true. Indeed, genuine confession can be an admission to more than has been charged: "You only know a part of what I said about you. It was worse than you think...."

In James 5:16, we are commanded to confess our sins to one another. There is no support here for the confessional. Nor is there any support for public confession of private sin. Matthew 18:15ff makes it clear that the confession ought to be made only as widely as the sin. In cases like that in Corinth, in which it was "commonly reported" that incest was going on, a common confession of sin and repentance was necessary. But to take James 5 as warrant for all sorts of encounter sessions in which one is encouraged to "spill his guts" to persons who are neither involved in the sin, nor should be, is totally unscriptural.

In the final analysis true confession is agreement with another that is in agreement with God's Word. One must never confess as sin what he is not sure, biblically, is sin. Nor should he confess to sins that he does not believe he has committed merely in order to appease another who has charged him with such wrongdoings. Confession must be the genuine, heartfelt conviction of the repentant confessor.

Forgiveness flows from confession like water flows from a spring. How often in counseling sessions have I seen a husband and wife melt into each other's arms in glad tears when finally confession is made and forgiveness is sought! How frequently I have heard one person say to another, with the profoundest sense of relief, "I didn't ever think I'd hear you admit to it! But I am so glad you did."

from FORGIVEN to forgiving

When one admits he is wrong and seeks forgiveness, nothing more stands in the way of his being forgiven; nothing more may be required. The promise to "remember no more" *must* be made.

12 FORGIVENESS AT WORK

ଉଓଉଓଉଓଉଓଉଓଉଓଉଓଉଓଉଓଉଓଉଓଉଓଉଓଉଓଉଓଉଓ

I n this chapter I plan to take up three typical instances to which the biblical principles of forgiveness may be applied, in order to show you how they work.

Forgiveness and Adultery

Walt committed adultery. He didn't mean to, but in a weak moment when things were not going well at work or at home, when he was feeling sorry for himself and when a woman in the neighborhood made herself available, well...he did. Now he has repented, confessed, and sought his wife's forgiveness. After some difficulty—tears, outbursts ("How could you?"), and the like—the pastor, calming her down, has helped Joanne to respond positively.

"I'll forgive him," Joanne says.

Two days later Joanne asks the pastor to pay a visit. That night as he sits before Walt and Joanne, the following conversation takes place.

Walt: Pastor, Joanne wants a divorce. I thought everything was settled and we could go on to reestablish our marriage on a more solid basis, like you said. Why, we

haven't even met with you for our first counseling session. I know it's been tough on her, but I just don't understand.

Pastor: Well, I'm certainly glad you called me right away. Joanne, is this how you see it? Has Walt got it right?

Joanne: Yes, he does. I just can't go on living with him! It's true that I've forgiven him, and as promised I won't keep bringing the matter up to him, but there's no way I can live with a man who did such a thing.

Pastor: I see. Well, first of all, let me help you out on one thing: In 1 Corinthians 10:13, God says that "there is no trial that has overtaken you but such as is common to man." That means that other Christians have faced this sort of thing successfully before you. And He goes on to say, "God is faithful who will not allow you to be tested beyond that which you are able to bear." That means that nothing comes your way that you can't handle, if you handle it His way. And He backs up this promise with His own faithfulness. That means that it is absolutely sure. Finally, He says, "With the trial, He will make a way of escape, in order that you may be able to bear it." By that, He means you will not remain under the pressures of the trial indefinitely; you can look forward to emerging from it successfully.

To sum it all up, what God is saying is that you can't say "can't"! Do you believe this promise—that He will never allow anything into your life that is beyond your ability to bear, presupposing, of course, that you deal with your problems biblically?

Joanne: Well...I guess I do, since that's what it says. But I still don't see how I could go on living with that man. He betrayed me! Besides...I don't have to. The Bible clearly says that I have a right to divorce him on the basis of adultery, doesn't it?

Pastor: Joanne, you have admitted that God can enable you to handle anything that comes your way. That's good!

And that means that if He requires you to reestablish this marriage on a firm, biblical basis, you *could* do so—right?

Joanne: I guess that's right, *if* He required it. But, as I told you, I don't have to. I've got clear grounds for divorce: he committed adultery! What about that?

Walt: How can she say she forgives me when she would turn around and divorce me? Pastor, I love her! How can I get that across to her? I'm really sorry for what I've done, and I mean it when I say I will work hard at becoming the kind of husband God wants me to be. Isn't there some way you can persuade her not to go through with this divorce?

Pastor: Walt, I was just about to deal with the question. But one thing at a time. It is important to establish first that God never requires His children to do anything He fails to give them both the wisdom and the strength to accomplish. Among other things, that's what 1 Corinthians 10:13 teaches. And, Joanne, you seem to understand that fact and accept it as true, if I hear you correctly—right?

Joanne: Yes I do, but you still haven't said anything about the fact that the Bible allows me to get a divorce on grounds of adultery. What about that?

Pastor: If I were able to show you that the passage that allows divorce doesn't apply to your case, and that, while it may be hard, it would be possible for you and Walt to have a marriage that sings by making it thoroughly biblical in all respects, you'd believe it possible to do so, wouldn't you?

Joanne: Well...I'm not sure. That seems pretty remote now. I guess, theoretically, I'd assent to it, but think of what he's done. It seems rather farfetched to believe that this marriage could be saved, let alone become a marriage that "sings."

Pastor: Good! You do admit that possibility then, no matter how slim? You do believe that it is not impossible for God to make your marriage a success?

Joanne: Yes...but...

Pastor: Then, let's consider the facts. Walt has repented of his sin, broken off the illicit relationship, asked your forgiveness, and says he is willing to do whatever God requires of him to make this marriage work. And he has said he's willing to attend regular counseling sessions with you and me to work on this. Right, Walt?

Walt: Definitely! There's nothing I want more. And I really mean it.

Pastor: Joanne, you forgave Walt. Right?

Joanne: That's true.

Pastor: Now, I explained to you what forgiveness means before you did, so that you would do so with understanding.

Joanne: You said it meant that I couldn't bring his sin up to Walt again. When I divorce him, it will be even easier to keep that promise. I won't have occasion to do so. Divorce should help out all around!

Pastor: Wait a minute. I'm afraid you've got it all wrong. I also talked about the fact that when you forgive a person, the promise "not to remember" means you won't *use* his sin against him. Divorce is both bringing up his sin and using it against him in a most vigorous way! And you'll also recall how we talked about forgiveness as the prelude to reconciliation?

Joanne: You mean I can't divorce him because I forgave him?

Pastor: Right!

Joanne: Then I shouldn't have made the promise. Can I take it back?

Pastor: No. You had no choice in the matter. When he repented and came to you asking forgiveness, you were required by the Bible to grant it. Remember Luke 17:3-4, where Jesus commands you to forgive him—seven times a day?

Joanne: Yes, I guess so.

Pastor: Do you see that God wants you to work on reestablishing this marriage on a new and better basis? That's why he gave us this wonderful process of forgiveness—so we could work out problems like this for His honor. By His grace, you can!

Walt: I sure want to. What do you say, Joanne?

Joanne: If there's no way out, I guess I'll have to. But I can tell you right now that I don't like it. I don't think it will work in our case. But if I have to go through with it, I'll give it what it takes, and Pastor, you're going to have to give us a lot of help. It isn't going to be easy, and I haven't the faintest idea where to begin.

Pastor: Joanne, you've already begun and so has Walt. I'm delighted to hear you talk that way. Of course I'll help you. That's why we've set up our first counseling session for tomorrow night. I'm anxious to show you how God can make it all happen.

This scenario should help you to understand the practicality of the principles you have been studying throughout this book. You can see that they come together in various ways to bring direction and help in time of confusion and uncertainty. That is why you must learn them, and learn to apply them as well. Now let's turn our attention to a very different situation.

Teaching Children to Forgive

How can forgiveness best be taught to children? It seems like you would be forcing them to utter words that they neither understand nor mean ("Ask for forgiveness, or I'll wallop you!"; "Say 'I forgive you,' or else!"), right? Well, if that's how you'd handle the teaching of forgiveness, you'd be sure to fail.

Should we force children to say things and make promises they don't really mean? Certainly not. Let's explore how it should be done.

There are two principal ways to go about it. First, you should teach in the milieu, as Deuteronomy 6 and 11 indicate. God's ways are to be taught and impressed on the hearts of your children when lying down, sitting up, walking, etc. That means in the course of the ordinary activities of life, whenever and wherever they occur. So, when an altercation between one of the children and another takes place, that's a good time to impress on them the importance of forgiveness. But *not until they are ready to hear*. That may mean waiting until they have calmed down, until you have been able to reason with them from the Bible and instruct them carefully in what they must do. No child should be forced to make promises he neither understands nor intends to keep. Nor should any child be forced to say he repents when he doesn't. That's the first point.

The second is every bit as important. Parents (school teachers, grandparents, etc.) will find that forgiveness is taught most impressively in the milieu *by example*. Because they are sinners, adults will wrong children from time to time. It is right for them to follow biblical principles and practices of confession ("I was wrong to punish you, Johnny. I now know that you didn't break the window.") and forgiveness ("Will you forgive me for being too hasty in condemning you?"). Nothing impresses the proper biblical obligations and procedures on a child more deeply than this. When little children see you practicing the principles of forgiveness, they will be anxious to do so themselves.

One should not seek forgiveness from a child merely as a teaching device, of course. That would be deception and hypocrisy. But if an adult who is zealous to please Christ has wronged a child, he will want to follow the biblical procedures with that child as soon as the child is able to understand. In doing so, *as a by-product,* the adult will instruct the child in the very best way—by example. Incidentally, there will be no lack of incidents in which the lesson may be genuinely taught!

"Doesn't asking children for forgiveness diminish a parent's or teacher's authority over them?"

No. Definitely not! Rather, it establishes it, and it does something else that is very important too. It is true that asking for forgiveness points away from the adult as the ultimate authority, and, instead, points to the authority of God. It demonstrates also that, while adults do have authority, it is derived and regulated by another: God's authority. Asking for forgiveness indicates most clearly that such adults do not consider themselves a law unto themselves, but that they themselves live under and submit to God's authority. That is good.

After all, the parent's goal should be to help children recognize the Bible as the ultimate standard for life and, at length, help them to judge all other authorities (including their own) by its precepts. The parent's task is to bring his child into willing, grateful submission to the Bible as early in life as possible. Seeking a child's forgiveness, when it is an act that has been fully explained in the light of the Cross, is one prime way to do so.

Misuse and Abuse

Consider a third scenario. Lois is in her mid-forties, divorced, with one teenage child. She is lonely. You are a happily married man in your early fifties. You are both members of the same church. You and Lois are on the same church committee.

One day Lois approaches your wife, saying, "Mildred, I have something dreadful to tell you. I believe your husband is in love with me. I have hesitated to tell you about this, but before it goes too far, I thought you'd better know."

Mildred, of course, is shocked. She asks for details. The answers she receives are fuzzy. "There have been innuendos," says Lois, "that any woman would understand. It's the way he looks at me, for one thing." When pressed, Lois cannot describe the look. "Well, it's also the inflec-

tion in his voice," she adds. Again, under pressure—nothing definite. "And he does take me home after committee meetings, you know."

Mildred asks, "Has he ever gone in or suggested doing so?"

The answer is a reluctant, "No...but I can tell he is thinking about it."

That night your wife confronts you with Lois' accusations. They come as a totally new thought. "Me? you ask. You are utterly innocent and dumbfounded, as Mildred can easily tell. You ask, "Mildred, you don't believe a word of this, do you?"

"Well, Phil," she replies, "I did wonder why she would come and confess all this if there was nothing to it."

"I don't believe this! I've never so much as made a pass at her! I can't remember ever speaking a word out of line that could be construed as a hint. I don't even think of her in any other way than a pitiful person. That's why I have tried to be kind to her. It's all in her head!"

What happens now? You've been wrongly accused. Your wife has been unnecessarily upset. At this point, many persons would approach Lois in a weak, unbiblical way, saying something like, "I'm sorry if I said or did anything to give you the idea that I was interested in you, Lois. Will you forgive me?"

But that is all wrong. You did nothing wrong. To ask Lois for forgiveness when you have done nothing wrong (with that all-too-frequent appendage, "*If* I did or said anything") is an abuse of the process of forgiveness. When you ask for forgiveness, be very sure that it is out of *repentance over sin*. To ask for forgiveness is always an admission of sin! Lois has wronged *you*. On the basis of her loneliness and desire to have male attention, she has built up a fantasy relationship totally in her own mind. It is she who must ask for forgiveness once she comes to acknowledge the true nature of the facts.

Now, of course, if you had done or said anything indiscreet—in jest or otherwise—you ought to seek forgiveness for *that*. But only if it was truly indiscreet. You must never ask forgiveness for error or wrongdoing on the part of another *in order to appease her*. All too often this ploy is used to relieve the tension, but it is a pretense and a sham. If you know you are not guilty, in effect you are willingly misrepresenting the situation in order to appease Lois.

What must be done then? You, your wife, and Lois must come to a clear understanding of the matter. You do not believe that you have sinned and believe the wrong is in Lois' interpretation of the facts. If your marriage is sound, Mildred will respond with love toward you expressed by "believing all things and hoping all things" (1 Cor. 13:7). She will surely stand with you in explicit trust, refusing to believe Lois on such flimsy evidence.

Together, you will confront Lois telling her that her suspicions are wrong. She must be rebuked for entertaining them on such a fanciful basis. You should say something like, "I never would have believed that my efforts to be kind and considerate would be taken for romantic interest. I want you to know, unequivocally, that there never has been anything in my mind beyond that."

If Lois breaks down, cries, admits that she has been wrong, and accepts the explanation as valid, that could end the matter. Even then Phil must be careful about future kindnesses, and he probably should arrange for another committee member to take Lois home.

Suppose Lois persists. Suppose she "knows" there was a good bit more to your kindness than mere Christian concern? What then? If you and Mildred cannot persuade her she is wrong and get her to accept your word, you may

have to call in one or two others, according to Matthew 18:16. Then the process of reconciliation through church discipline begins.

The key point is *you must never use forgiveness as a gimmick.*

Weak, confusing signals are set by those who use forgiveness to placate another, even when they know they are not at fault. If you followed the "Will you forgive me if..." line, you would allow Lois to "save face." But does she really need an out? Is it right for her to save face? Surely not at the expense of the truth. Indeed Lois needs to face up to her problem and, if necessary, get counsel from her pastor about letting her imagination run wild. After all, she has disquieted you and your wife. She should be seeking forgiveness for this.

Forgiveness is the wonderful God-given remedy for sin. It must never be cheapened by using it for lesser purposes.

From these three concrete life circumstances you can see both the importance and the practicality of forgiveness. You see how it works, how it may be taught, and how important it can be in the home and the church. You also see something of how to avoid its abuse.

Forgiveness is not an option. It is not something that would be nice to do. It is an important factor in the life of the Christian. No matter if others around you do not understand. Begin to practice the principles of forgiveness yourself, and you will instruct others as well as reap the benefits in your own life.

13 THE CHURCH AS A FORGIVING COMMUNITY

ᖇᏫᎥᖇᏫᎥᖇᏫᎥᖇᏫᎥᖇᏫᎥᖇᏫᎥᖇᏫᎥᖇᏫᎥᖇᏫᎥᖇᏫᎥᖇᏫᎥᖇᏫᎥᖇᏫᎥᖇᏫᎥᖇᏫᎥᖇᏫᎥᖇᏫᎥᖇᏫᎥ

It seems, sometimes, that the world is more forgiving than the church. Frequently such accusations are made. People outside the church seem to take sin in stride, we are told, whereas the church calls attention to it, judges it, and often becomes judgmental in doing so. How is that? What is really happening?

In thinking through this phenomenon, let me first make an important distinction. We can talk about the church as it *ought to be* or the church as it *often is*. In those unwelcome comparisons the church is described in the latter mode rather than the former. But the church as it often is, is comprised of numbers of persons who themselves are forgiven but have yet a long way to go to approximate the biblical ideals that make the church what it ought to be.

Congregations dominated by those who do not adequately understand God's requirements or have difficulty obeying them, tend to act like the world itself or in strange, legalistic, and (sometimes) pharisaical ways. It is this about which people comment unfavorably.

Let's forget all such unbiblical aberrations of the church and talk about the church at her best—when she more nearly

thinks and acts as God intended. At times she does, you know. It is then she will be a forgiving community in the proper, biblical sense of the word.

A forgiving community is made up of forgiven people who have not forgotten that fact. In pharisaical and legalistic communities, people have forgotten that it is only by the grace of God they are what they are. Or they find it possible to pretend they are better than they really are by conforming outwardly to biblical standards. Unless they are jogged from time to time by powerful and precise preaching, such communities gradually acquire the notion that they did not need forgiving all that much when they were saved—just minimally! But congregations at their best are composed of grateful people who do remember the pit from which they were rescued (Isa. 51:1). They act neither shocked by sin in others nor superior to those in whom sin is found.

"Well, that's how the world acts too, isn't it? What's the difference?"

When examined closely you will find the two approaches significantly different. The world is not a forgiving community; it is a condoning one. The word "acceptance" much more closely describes the world's attitude than "forgiveness." There is a large difference between the two attitudes.

"I don't see it. Aren't the two essentially the same? After all, these days Christians always seem to be writing and talking about accepting people, don't they?"

Though many Christians have confused the matter by using *acceptance* inaccurately, as virtually synonymous with forgiveness, the two words are actually opposites. Acceptance is a nonjudgmental reception of a person as he is; it amounts to condoning sin. Forgiveness, on the contrary, judges each one, calling sin "sin," refusing to condone sin or ignore it but gladly forgiving it on repentance. There is all the difference there could be between these two approaches to sinners.

Jesus is often (wrongly) called an "accepting" Person and Christians are urged to imitate Him in this respect. Applied to Jesus, the appellation grossly distorts the truth about Him. While Jesus was preeminently forgiving, He never accepted, ignored, or condoned sin. Typical of His attitude are the statements, "Your sins are forgiven you" and "Go and sin no more." Jesus *forgave* sinners; He never accepted them as they were. To do so would have denied the very purpose of His coming to take away the sins of the world and would have made the Cross a futile, cruel mistake.

"But doesn't He hate the sin and love the sinner?"

That is a very misleading slogan that has absolutely no biblical basis. Rather, the wrath of God hangs over the head of guilty, unforgiven *sinners.* Answer me this: What does God punish everlastingly in hell—sin or sinners? It is impossible to detach one from the other. Sin is not some sort of substance that you could spread on bread like peanut butter. You can't really talk about sin in and of itself because sins are acts done against God and wrong attitudes of persons held toward God and their neighbors.

It is certainly easier to ignore or condone sin than to forgive it. Doubtless, that is why the world adopts this stance. Those who ignore or condone sin need make no judgment about the sinner. Those who forgive hold him guilty, rebuke him, call him to repentance, and on confession of sin, promise never to bring up the matter again. Forgivers, in contrast to condoners, become deeply involved with the sinner—at the very point of his sin. They seek to do him good at great cost to themselves. Forgiving is not easy; it costs. Unquestionably, even many Christians shy away from the process of forgiveness and adopt other measures for this very reason.

Just because forgiveness is so thorough and deals definitively with transgressions, reconciliation is possible. A solid foundation for reconciliation is laid, embarrassing matters are never raised again, and the forgiven and the forgiving are free to go on together *as if the sin never occurred.*

Obstacles to fellowship are removed by forgiveness. In contrast, the world's way of ignoring, condoning, and accepting sin means that nothing has been settled. Down deep, offenses still rankle. Real fellowship and communion are not possible where repressed resentments and suspicion fester. The offender, on his part, continues to bear the load of unforgiven sin and guilt. The burden has not been lifted and the commitment never to remember the matter against him again has not been made. The threat that his sin will be used against him continuously dangles over his head. You can see, therefore, how utterly different forgiveness is from acceptance.

Awareness of this difference and the contrast involved in it should make the Christian community much more careful to pursue its privilege and obligation to forgive. But how does the Christian community, *as a community*, forgive?

Corporate Forgiveness

While forgiveness is primarily an individual matter, the Bible does recognize corporate forgiveness. This is forgiveness by the church *as a whole, as an organized body of believers.* Speaking to the church of Corinth as a church, Paul wrote, "Now, when you forgive somebody for something, I forgive him too" (2 Cor. 2:10).

This is corporate forgiveness. The power of corporate forgiveness was given to the church by the Lord Jesus Himself. "If you forgive anyone's sins, they are forgiven them; if you retain them, they are retained" (John 20:23). Reading these words as a fulfillment of Christ's promise, to give

His church disciplinary authority (Matt. 16:18, 18:18), it becomes clear that such disciplinary authority included the task of determining whether to grant or withhold corporate forgiveness, having to do with entrance or, as here, reentrance into the body on determination of one's repentance and faith. Peter and the apostles received such authority directly from the Lord for the church of all ages. In the Corinthian situation, Paul did not forgive, but urged the congregation to do so. He thereby indicated that such authority belonged not to the apostles, as such, but was given to them as representatives of the church at a time when, apart from the apostolic band, the New Testament church did not exist in an organized form. This authority was so important that Jesus did not wait until Pentecost, but conferred it immediately after His resurrection.

A repentant sinner who had previously been put out of the church because he would not repent of his sin was now seeking readmission into the body. His sin was against the congregation, an insidious leaven that might have leavened the whole lump (1 Cor. 5:6) had not Paul insisted on the application of church discipline. Scandalous conditions existed in which the Corinthian church pursued the world's policy of acceptance. The church condoned incest on the part of one of its members (1 Cor. 5:1-13). Paul's scathing rebuke of the church for its acceptance got results. The church handed the offender over to Satan (i.e., they put him out of the realm of protection in the visible kingdom of God into the domain of Satan), and the man repented eventually. How should his application for readmission into the church be handled? It seems as if there were various opinions among the members of the Corinthian church. So Paul explained in detail what God requires in such a case:

1. Forgive him.
2. Official (or formally) reinstate him.
3. Give him whatever assistance he may need in making reentry.

The first of these requirements, forgiveness, involves both a corporate and an individual act. We read in 2 Corinthians 2:10 how first the body as a whole, then Paul as an individual, forgave the offender. What Paul did was what every individual in the church must also do. But he was setting the example.

The second requirement was to render such assistance as the forgiven brother needed to become reestablished in the body. The Greek word used for "comfort" in verse 7 is very broad, but at its core is the idea of assisting another in whatever ways may be necessary (by comfort, encouragement, persuasion, counsel, etc.). After being handed over to Satan, this brother may return to the church battered, bruised, and buffeted. He may even need financial help or physical care and nurture. Satan can be very rough on such deserters who return to his domain. In all instances, the returning brother will need assistance in becoming reassimilated. Reentry can be difficult for everyone. We know how difficult it was for Paul to become fully assimilated into the church after his conversion because of suspicion and so on. But Barnabas, who was called "the son of assistance," eased the way. Something like this must be done in cases of reassimilation as well.

The third requirement was clearly a corporate act in which (as the word "reaffirm" in the original language means) the repentant sinner was to be formally reinstated to full, loving communion in the church, with all its rights and privileges. The word, occurring only there in the New Testament, indicates a formal act done by a body in such a way that the person to whom it is done is fully reinstated into the position that he held before he was put out of it. Of course, the formal, official act of the church as a body was to be accepted by each individual member, who would be required to treat the reinstated member as a first-class citizen of the kingdom of God. No one had the right to avoid him, treat him as a second-class citizen, or withhold his love from him. Through forgiveness and reaffirmation of love the church once again acknowledges a repentant member who has been put out of the church as a brother—a member of the visible, organized church in good standing.

Forgiveness is what makes the other two requirements viable. Apart from forgiveness, reinstatement and reassimilation are not possible; indeed, they would be sin. That is probably why Paul mentions forgiveness first and refers to the whole process under the rubric of forgiveness in verse 10. Be that as it may, until and unless the church has lifted one's guilt and has promised not to remember his sin against him, neither reentry assistance nor reaffirmation may take place.

Forgiveness by a body must be done by the officers in the name of Christ and His church. Not only should they go on record to the forgiven one himself (verbally, and the word would indicate the probable need for a written affirmation as well), but the elders should also explain to the entire congregation exactly what is transpiring and the implications of forgiveness, assistance, and the reaffirmation of love. Each member should be encouraged to express his or her own assent to the act of corporate forgiveness by welcoming the returning brother and by rendering him whatever assistance possible. Members should also make an effort to reestablish and express new brotherly relationships to the forgiven one. The elders would be wise to warn any who are indisposed to do these things that if they are found treating him as a second-class citizen, they themselves may become subject to church discipline.

In other words, when the church corporately forgives, each member must also follow through. As a layman, you should be ready to do so whenever the occasion arises.

14 OBSTACLES TO FORGIVENESS

In this chapter, we won't be dealing with the well understood obstacles of stubborness, pride, and the like. While these are formidable obstacles that can sometimes only be removed by church discipline, most persons reading this book would be able to identify them rather easily. However, there are more subtle obstacles that even readers acquainted with the biblical process of forgiveness, and anxious to follow it, may encounter. In attempting to do so they may find these either perplexing or too formidable, unless they are exposed in their true light as obstacles and the way around them is expressly set forth. It is with two such obstacles that I wish to deal at this time.

Healing of the Memories

The concept and practice of the "healing of the memories" has become widespread. Various forms of memory "healing" are articulated and used. Often some sort of exorcism accompanies the process. Whatever form it may take, without a doubt the central idea that unpleasant memories can be erased by "healing" them has obtained wide acceptance in Christian circles. Is such a practice Christian, and what relationship does it bear to biblical forgiveness?

To begin with, the concept that memories can be "healed" strikes me as strange, if not weird. How can memories get "sick" and need healing? The very notion may repulse some. But others with unpleasant memories lay hold on the promises of those who advocate such healing in order to obtain relief. Some are disappointed. Others, who may experience some form of relief, at length may discover that they have been duped by well-meaning but misguided persons into following a course of action that only conceals problems rather than dealing with them in a thoroughly biblical fashion. As a result they will find that unpleasant memories will return, accompanied by others that have been added to them making the problem even worse.

The concept and practice of "healing memories" is not merely a strange system, it is a very dangerous one as well. What makes it so serious is that it becomes a substitute for, and thus an obstacle to, God's true, scriptural way of dealing with the past through forgiveness.

Instead of following biblical principles of confrontation, repentance, confession, forgiveness, and reconciliation, the memory healer encourages the one seeking healing to mentally relive past unpleasant events, while visualizing Jesus in the experience making all go well. Sometimes He is to be visualized as walking hand in hand with the "patient" through the experience, assuring him or her that His healing presence will extract the bad effects from the experience. Healing of the memories thus becomes a Christianized form of desensitization.

There is nothing in the Bible about any such process. That is the first trenchant point to be made. Of course the Bible doesn't speak of everything, but when Jesus is the

subject of any process or system, those who propagate it had better be very sure that what they teach is unmistakably biblical. Otherwise by including Him in their system they may misrepresent Him and teach, as Christian, views and doctrines that are not Christian at all. As a matter of fact, that is exactly what has happened in the recent rise of this method. As a result principles and practices of forgiveness, which unquestionably are taught in the Bible, either have been replaced, redefined, weakened, or eliminated altogether. This is a serious fault.

Moreover, this self-centered focus, in which the one with the bad memories is the sole concern, has nothing to say of the one who offended. So long as the bad feelings of the offended one are relieved, all is well. That's all that really counts. The offender, whether it be a father who abused his daughter as a little girl, or an employer who cheated the "patient" out of a large sum of money, is ignored. Little or no concern is shown for the offender. There is no love reaching out in this. The biblical priorities of relieving him of his guilt through forgiveness and becoming reconciled to him in the future are not in the picture. Instead, self-absorption reaches its height in the process.

Those who understand and practice biblical forgiveness have no need of unbiblical visualization techniques. For nearly two thousand years Christians have found that, as a by-product, unpleasant memories are erased when they follow the express words of Scripture. One wonders how believers got along before the last twenty years or so when these new, "important discoveries" were made and these practices were begun!

Healing of the memories is a dangerous, inadequate substitute for the real thing. It is dangerous in that it leaves unforgiven and unreconciled the relationships of persons who thereby remain in wrong relationship to God as well.

It is inadequate in that it fails to resolve the real problem underlying bad memories—lack of forgiveness.

Christians who follow biblical injunctions for dealing with problems know that making and keeping the promise of forgiveness, incidentally (not as its main purpose, but as a by-product) also solves the memory problem. When one no longer brings up a matter to an offender, to anyone else, or even to himself, according to the promise "not to remember," he discovers that forgetting occurs more rapidly and more completely than he expected.

When he builds a new relationship with the offender, made possible only by forgiveness, and begins to see in him works appropriate to his repentance, focus on the forgiven brother or sister's past wrongdoings is replaced by pleasure and gratitude arising from his present righteous acts and attitudes.

In every way, then, this modern trend proves to be not only extrabiblical, but also a substitute for forgiveness, an obstacle to pursuing God's straight paths to righteousness.

Modern Psychology

Just as healing of the memories—one application of Wolpe's psychological desensitization program—becomes an obstacle to biblical forgiveness, psychology's general views of man, God, and values prove also to be an enormous obstacle.

A few years back, Karl Menninger, dean of American psychotherapists, wrote a truly amazing book entitled *Whatever Became of Sin?* It is remarkable because in it Menninger, himself no evangelical Christian, contends that the disappearance of the concept of sin over the period of his long lifespan has occasioned a corresponding malaise in society that he believes is the result of this decline. He thinks that there are many persons who are wrongly labeled

sick or criminal. If these people were to be rightly labeled and treated as "sinners," they would be capable of being forgiven and thus healed of various disorders.

Menninger claims that over his lifespan he watched the shrinking and eventual demise of the category of "sin" as both government and psychiatry encroached on Christianity, relabeling first this sin and then that a "crime" or a "sickness." (Notice that is exactly what the healing of memories people have done: They have imposed on what the Bible considers a matter of sin and forgiveness an alternate explanation that focuses on sickness.) This problem has grown so serious, says Mennigner, that it is now necessary to ask, "Is no one any longer guilty of anything?"[35]

Menninger rightly discerns that both criminal prevention and rehabilitation as well as psychotherapy have been proven inadequate as solutions to those problems that previously were, and now ought to be, considered sins. That failure, he asserts, comes from the fact that there is no other way to deal with sin than by forgiveness.

Menninger's recognition of the impoverishment of Western society resulting from the abandonment of the category of sin is not only overdue but startlingly refreshing. Yet even though the book has been in circulation for some twenty years, it is strange that Christians have ignored Menninger's call for a return to a recognition of sin. It is true that when Menninger spells out what he means by sin, atonement, and forgiveness, he does so in disappointingly humanistic terms. His call for a return is, therefore, only a new departure in directions that again, if followed, would be a substitute for God's truth. But he is right in his general observations about the shrinking of the concept of sin and the need for a return to forgiveness as the remedy to many of the problems of modern man.

Menninger has raised the problem of labeling. Labels are important not only as signs of the thing they signify but also as signposts that point to solutions to the problems they categorize. When a drunkard is labeled "sick," according to modern psychological propaganda, rather than "sinful," according to clear biblical teaching, you will tend to send him to a physician rather than to a pastor for a solution to his problem. Even many pastors, so heavily brainwashed in seminaries and by the books published by Christians who are psychologists, have tended to follow and propagate such errors in spite of Scripture. As a whole they have become ineffective in using the Bible to counter the insidious problem of drink. If drunkenness is a sickness (not that it can't lead to sickness), so is cocaine abuse!

When a husband sinfully abuses his wife, instead of thinking of forgiveness, reconciliation, and change, his sinful activity is counted a crime or sickness and he is incarcerated in a jail or a mental ward. The result is that the family is even more greatly broken by his departure with all of the evils attending that, rather than reconciled to him in forgiveness, helping him under pastoral guidance to overcome his sinful practices by biblical ways and means.

Another evil stemming from the demise of the concept of sin and its replacement by psychiatric explanations has begun to be recognized by thinking Christians. Now when a brother approaches an offending brother, according to our Lord's directions in Matthew 18:15, he is as likely as not to find the response to his well-intentioned rebuke is, "Oh, I'm sorry it happened, but you see, I have this emotional problem that from time to time causes me to act that way. I just had a need to..."

The offending brother refuses to assume personal responsibility for his behavior and, therefore, logically recognizes no need for repentance, confession of sin, or seeking forgiveness.

On the other side, the obligation to go to the one who wronged you and seek to be reconciled can just as readily be bypassed by claiming that the offender "just couldn't help it; it wouldn't do any good because he has a psychological

problem." The inevitable result is that sins—genuine violations of God's law—are redefined and excused; repentance, confession, and forgiveness are bypassed; and the brother who was wronged is left without recourse. Or on the other hand the wrongdoer is left in his sin and guilt, unforgiven, with all the dire consequences that arise from unforgiven sin. The devil has found a way, through psychotherapeutic terminology and categories, to effectively neutralize Matthew 18!

If the offended brother appeals to one or two others (Matt. 18:15ff) they, also being brainwashed by psychological propagandists, are more than likely to agree with the sinner's assessment of the situation and excuse his sin as an "emotional problem." If he carries the matter to the church, unless the pastor is one of those growing number of men who, becoming weary of the Scriptures being overridden by psychology, practices fully biblical counseling procedures, it is altogether possible that he will hear the same thing from the elders and the pastor.

The processes leading to forgiveness have been effectively blocked by psychiatric obstructions. And as a result forgiveness, in many cases, has been rendered nugatory.

What can be done about this problem? Obviously the person sinned not because he "had a need" to do so. He sinned because he is a sinner. First, you must recognize the truth of the situation. That is where any solution must begin. You cannot hesitate and be turned off by excuses and as a result neglect your duty as it is spelled out in Matthew 18:15ff. Then, you must instruct others. Books, tapes, courses, and on-sight instruction in truly biblical counseling that recognizes sin as sin, and shows how to deal with problems through forgiveness are now available. This writer has published over forty books on various aspects of the subject. Materials like these will instruct you in the way to go and will provide help for those who are yet confused about the matter. Perhaps you will have to instruct those who should have been helping you.

Sometimes it is necessary to take matters to denominational officers of the church at a higher level for a more objective approach and where there may be persons who accept biblical rather than psychological categories. In independent congregations, when all else has failed, it still may be possible to enlist the pastor from another congregation to express a more biblical viewpoint to your pastor. But, above all, you must *do all God requires you to do* in the situation. Do not let down on your own obligations because someone else believes unbiblical teaching. God expects you to follow His requirements for you in your relationships to others regardless of how others respond. In the final analysis remember that the ideas of men are no obstruction to God. He can break through them in response to prayer and faithful action on your part, as if they were no more than the flimsiest cobwebs.

15 DANGEROUS SHORTCUTS, PLOYS, & EVASIONS

ෲෲෲෲෲෲෲෲෲෲෲෲෲෲෲෲෲෲෲෲ

It is in man's fallen nature to try another way. Though they have been given the ability to live differently, Christians still retain many of the old ways developed before salvation and carry them over into their Christian lives. These surface as substitutes or shortcuts offered in place of the ways of God revealed in Scripture. These shortcuts are always dangerous because they are nothing less than ways of circumventing God's commandments. In addition, human shortcuts never achieve what God wants accomplished; instead they aggravate the situation and usually bring about new and different evils.

As discussed earlier in chapter one, apologizing is the most common modern substitute for seeking forgiveness. Its prevalence among Christians, who don't seem to recognize that it is not an equivalent to forgiveness, makes it a prime example of how Christians can unknowingly circumvent God's forgiveness requirement by adopting the world's ways. By no means is apologizing the only way people try to avoid seeking or granting forgiveness. In this brief chapter we will be exploring other means of forgiveness avoidance.

As we become aware of this tendency to avoid forgiving, we can be alert to finding it in ourselves and in others.

Minimizing the Offense

Perhaps the most common ploy, other than the tactic of apologizing, is minimizing the offense. When you confess your sin and seek forgiveness from one whom you have wronged, you are told, "oh, there's really nothing to forgive." The person says this piously, as though he or she had not been offended in the least by what you did. He or she acts as though the relationship between the two of you were as sound as it could be when every action or word since the offense has indicated otherwise. He or she talks now as if no offense had occurred.

Why would someone deny being offended? What the person may want is to punish you by forcing you to retain the burden of your guilt, or the person may wish to make it possible to avoid the future relationship with you that he or she knows reconciliation through forgiveness would entail. Often this seeming expression of kindness and goodwill is really just a put-off!

What do you, as a guilt-laden sinner, who wants to be rid of this burden, do then?

Try to respond this way, "Well, I'm certainly glad to hear that! The load of my sin has been weighing me down. Since you don't consider the offense all that serious, I'm sure you won't mind forgiving me for my sake. It will mean a lot to me to know that you have promised neither to bring up nor to hold the matter against me in the future."

If what the offended one says were true, he or she would have absolutely no hesitancy or difficulty in saying, "I forgive you." But when confronted by you, the minimizer is likely to show his or her true colors very quickly either by refusing to make the promise (in which case you may be forced to pursue the course laid out in Matt. 18:15ff) or by further evasive ploys (each of which you should meet by

gently but firmly insisting upon biblical forgiveness). Minimizers will tell you that there is virtually no problem because they want the "right" to continue to talk to others about what you have done, and they want to have a reason to go on avoiding you in the future. God will not have this. He wants matters cleared up entirely and quickly. The only method whereby one may truly accomplish this is forgiveness. The minimizing shortcut will not do.

Understanding the Offense

Ever since modern psychologists revived it in one form or another, the old saying "To know all is to forgive all" has become the banner of many Christians. As the result, you will read books and articles by Christians that recommend "understanding" at points where the Bible requires forgiveness. Thus understanding ("knowing all") becomes a shortcut around forgiveness. While seeming to encourage forgiveness this catchy aphorism actually does the opposite. What it amounts to is this: When you come to understand another's motives, situation , background, etc., you won't even need to *forgive* him; you will realize why he did what he did and *excuse* him.

Given the sinful propensities of another, if you actually did understand, you might find it not easier but far more difficult to forgive. Indeed, you would probably want to rebuke the person for many other things you didn't know about! It's important to realize that God, the One who does know all (the only One who ever could) practices forgiveness and nothing else. Knowing all, it is He who has required forgiveness of us.

Author David Augsburger claims that one must understand another in order to forgive him. Somehow, this "understanding" is to separate what a person does from what a persons is. That is of course an unscriptural view of man. God never holds *deeds* responsible but the persons who do the deeds. He sends sinners, not sins, to hell. But listen to the excuse-laden language of David Augsburger, "If he is demanding, possessive, or even exploiting, he may be a little lost boy grasping desperately for affection and acceptance. Who could know? Maybe he is a victim of his own heredity or environment."[36]

Who would want to rebuke such a nonresponsible victim and insist that he repent and seek forgiveness? Why, all you'd want to do is cuddle him! Can't you see the demeaning nature of that approach which virtually excuses the sinners as a victim rather than a violator? It makes the person something less than a responsible human being who must face up to his or her sinful behavior and seek forgiveness. The heading of the section from which the preceding quotation was taken is entitled, "Understanding the Other." Yet, later in the same section Augsburger writes, "Don't try to understand the other person. Try, instead, to be understanding."

What exactly is meant here? In my mind to be understanding is to try to understand. How confused people become when they try to walk all around the simple biblical command to forgive. God never calls on us to understand in order to forgive. Presumably, Augsburger recognized what others who insist on understanding are doing is excusing people for their sin, so he made an untenable distinction between "trying to understand" and "being understanding." Possibly he did so because he was reluctant to leave behind the psychological approach which insists on understanding. Rather than abandon that unscriptural idea altogether, he reinterpreted it in the contradictory and unbiblical way I have noted.

Sin must never be excused, minimized, or reinterpreted as someone else's fault. Often, the person who quotes the aphorism "To know all is to forgive all," is the same person who wants to excuse himself and others of sin, blaming it on poor training by parents, squalid conditions in childhood, failure to receive the proper strokes when growing

up, or low self-esteem. Not only does God hold people guilty of their sin, regardless of conditions, but He expects us to do so too—especially as it relates to ourselves! He will not let us beg off by casting the blame on others. That ploy is as old as Adam and Eve. God knows that sin can be definitively dealt with in only one way—by forgiveness. God does not insist on forgiveness because He is some old ogre demanding His pound of flesh but because He loves His children. He knows that nothing else relieves the conscience, nothing else restores the relationship as does forgiveness. Therefore He requires forgiveness leading to entire reconciliation, nothing less.

The danger in substituting understanding (excusing) for forgiveness is twofold. First, the offender is not cleared, but his behavior is excused. That is to say, he "gets away with" his sin on the human level. This may harden him to sin by searing his conscience, or it may burden him by forcing him to go on carrying a load of unforgiven sin. Second, the offended one is allowed to go on talking about the wrongdoing, bringing it up to the offender in various ways. ("Well, you know, John, you've always been that way. You remember when...")

The offended one might also use the sin against him as an excuse for not becoming reconciled. "Well, that's just the way Mary is. I don't hold it against her, poor thing! She was raised that way, you know. But I certainly don't find her pleasant company to associate with!"

Because the offender is excused (perhaps again and again for the same wrong), he or she is offered no help to overcome the sin. You don't do that when you believe another is not responsible for his sin and incapable of changing.

"It Wouldn't Be Submissive"

Another way by which some seek to avoid forgiveness and reconciliation is to invoke and misuse the biblical command to be submissive to an authority. A child may refuse to rebuke a parent even though Luke 17:3 and Matthew 18:15 require it even of him. A wife may refuse to rebuke a husband, or an employee an employer, on the basis that to do so would be a breach of the biblical command to submit. For some this may be simple misunderstanding, but for others the misuse of this command is but a shrewd ploy to avoid an unpleasant and difficult responsibility.

At first it might seem wrong to rebuke one who has authority over you. But no such qualification of the command is ever given in the Scriptures. When you think about it, you should realize that rebuking with a view to being reconciled (the only sort that the Bible countenances) is an attempt to cement relationships even more closely. Realize that forgiveness has nothing to do with submission. A submission context is an authority relationship that involves two elements: respect and obedience. See, for example, 1 Peter 3:1-6 and Ephesians 5:21-33.

A child, employee, or wife can remain respectful and continue to obey all biblical requirements while confronting another about his or her wrongdoing. In the long run nothing shows more respect or more faithfulness than doing so! Of course the authority may or may not see it in that light. He or she may not be willing to acknowledge the wrongdoing, may become angry, and may misuse his or her authority in a harmful way that inflicts new injuries on you. But that is a separate matter. Your task is not to anticipate results and thereby determine whether or not to obey God's command; you must obey God regardless of the outcome.

Again, if the authority who responds this way is your brother or sister in Christ, you may find it necessary to pursue the course laid out in Matthew 18:15ff until, with the help of the church, matters are resolved God's way.

This example makes it clear that the confrontation, repentance, confession, and forgiveness dynamic is not without risk. Indeed, it can even involve suffering and loss.

[131]

But God does not expect you to disobey Him because of
possibly unfavorable consequences. Especially He does
not want you playing one command of His against another:
"I can't rebuke my teacher because that would not be submissive." God's commandments, rightly interpreted, never
conflict. God has His way of righting wrongs. Leave the
ultimate outcome to Him. Your task is not to try to determine what the responses of other persons will be; it is simply to obey—even when forgiveness costs. Don't forget, it
cost God His Son to forgive you.

"He Already Knows"

Usually you will encounter this next evasion among husbands and wives, family members, and close friends. When
you ask someone to make the promise to remember your
sin no more (i.e., to forgive you), he may object, "You already know that I have forgiven you. I don't have to go
through the ritual of saying so." Ever hear a husband say
something like that to his wife? However he does have to
"go through the ritual." All such answers (and they may
take many distinct forms) are evasive. While seeming to
say one thing, they really say another.

No one *can* know that another has forgiven him unless
that other person actually says so. That is true because of
the very nature of forgiveness. By its nature, a promise is
made, and it is always made (spoken, or given) to another.
So unless a promise is made to *someone*, there has been no
promise. The nature of a promise is that it involves at least
two parties, one of whom declares to the other that he or
she will or will not do (or stop doing) something. Promises
are not made out of the blue. If God had kept His willingness to forgive to Himself, instead of going on record in the
Bible, you could never be sure that you were forgiven. If,
in order to forgive you, God had to say so, you and I must
do so too. Willingness to forgive—though proper, neces-

sary, and commendable—is not forgiveness. A promise must be made.

These and all such ploys and evasions of forgiveness may not be tolerated. When insisting on forgiveness—the "ritual of forgiveness," if you will—be sure you do so in a kind, loving manner. It is altogether possible that the other person is merely ignorant of what you now know from reading this book. He or she may *not* be attempting to shortcut the biblical process, and with a kind explanation of the facts, may gladly assent. Indeed, the person may even be grateful for the instruction. You can always tell him you were reading this book and blame your "overly cautious" behavior in this matter on me!

Above all, attempt never to leave a forgiveness situation, regardless of which side of the wrongdoing you may be on, without the certainty that: (1) forgiveness and not some substitute has been granted, and (2) all parties involved understand exactly what forgiveness is and what responsibilities are involved in it. You may find it necessary to instruct others about the ins and outs of forgiveness to be sure that the transaction has been pursued biblically.

16 FORGIVENESS: HORIZONTAL & VERTICAL

ᴎᴑ

This book has dealt much with man-to-man relationships. That, of course, is the concern of the book—forgiven persons forgiving one another. Because most books about forgiveness have rather to do with the forgiveness of man by God, a book about person-to-person forgiveness is needed. But in a real sense this book is not about your relationships with your fellow men—at least, not only or primarily that. Fundamentally this book is about your relationship with God. It is concerned with obedience to the living God who tells His children to forgive one another, just as He has forgiven them.

I say this not simply because parental forgiveness with God the Father depends on willingness to forgive your brothers and sisters in the family. That, of course, is a significant factor in your relationship with God as Christ's emphasis in the Lord's Prayer indicates. The prayer for forgiveness, *"Forgive us our debts as we forgive our debtors"* (Matt. 6:12) and the footnote to the entire prayer, *"For if you forgive men for their transgressions, your Heavenly Father will also forgive you. But if you do not forgive men, then your Father will not forgive your transgressions"*

[134]

(Matt. 6:14-15), show the significance of the matter since this is the only item in the Lord's Prayer that is conditional and the only one amplified and explained in a footnote.

However, there is a more foundational issue with which we should be concerned here. That is the place of God Himself in man-to-man forgiveness. God is so central, that unbelievers cannot forgive.

Why Can't Non-Christians Forgive?

It was noted earlier that true, biblical, God-honoring forgiveness is possible only for those who themselves have been the subjects of God's forgiveness. Believers alone can obey the command to be kind, "forgiving one another, just as God, in Christ has forgiven you" (Eph. 4:32, NASB).

It should be obvious that those who have never experienced forgiveness and reconciliation following true repentance (in which they abandon their own thoughts and ways in favor of God's) can never forgive others in a similar manner. That is why, for unbelievers, forgiveness becomes apologizing on the one hand and accepting an apology on the other. That's why liberals so easily confuse forgiveness with "'an attitude of acceptance,' in which one reacts 'to harm, not with hostility which hurts both parties, but with love which affirms the best in both persons.'"[37] They claim that, in forgiveness, one must "accept those who hurt us."[38]

Nothing could be further from the truth. Rather than accept others in their sin, the person who is willing to forgive *confronts* the offender about it, rebukes him for it, and endeavors in every loving, biblically legitimate way to induce him to confess it as wrong and turn from it. That is the very opposite of acceptance. Did Jesus ever "accept" people as they were? Of course not; He always changed them. God did not accept you as you were when He saved you. You were so bad He had to send His Son to die for you. Having regenerated you by His Spirit, He is now in

[135]

the process of refashioning you into the image of Christ. The weak, liberal position that takes acceptance for forgiveness also weakens the *act* of promising not the remember to a mere attitude of goodwill. Carol Wise, for instance, says that forgiveness is, "not so much an act, as an attitude, a relationship."[39] While attitudes are present, and important, and relationships are at stake, forgiveness is neither.

Clearly as this example notes, those who have never experienced God's forgiveness must reinterpret it in everyday, worldly categories (e.g., apologizing) or in psychological ones (e.g., acceptance). The Christian looks at forgiveness quite differently. God, the Spirit, is *in* our forgiveness of one another, enabling us to understand all about forgiveness from the Bible and encouraging us by that Word to seek and grant that kind of forgiveness.

Pope's famous aphorism, "To err is human, to forgive divine," is, then, partially true. While Christians can truly forgive, even they cannot do so *apart* from divine revelation, illumination, and motivation. In all three of these, the Holy Spirit is active using the Book He Himself spent long years inspiring and through which He now works.

Vertical and Horizontal Dimensions

John Murray makes the point that the sin we forgive is not sin against God—only He can forgive that—but are those injuries that are against us.[40] Naturally all sin, even against us (sin with a horizontal dimension), is also vertical (sin against God). That is because He has forbidden us to transgress against one another and commanded us rather to love and do good to one another. To do what God forbids or to fail to do what He commands is sin—sin against God. That is why God's forgiveness, *as well as* man's, must always be sought. It is never sufficient to ask man alone to forgive. Because unbelievers do not know the true God, they not only cannot forgive, but they cannot be truly forgiven. They have no right to God's parental forgiveness. Since they are not a part of His family of faith, they are never truly forgiven even if a believer should be willing to grant them his forgiveness

Until they turn in repentance to Jesus Christ as Saviour and receive judicial forgiveness from God, at best non-Christians can be forgiven only on the horizontal dimension. Even then, because it is partial, misunderstood, and misappropriated forgiveness, the horizontal forgiveness is virtually useless to an unbeliever. He may even use it to confirm himself in his rejection of God ("Well, now that I've made things right with Bill, I'm OK").

Murray points out that God must forgive sin against Himself. We do not, therefore, forgive sin, considered as the breaking of God's commandments, but only as it is considered injurious to ourselves. Many of the older writers attempting to distinguish horizontal forgiveness from vertical forgiveness, speak of human-to-human forgiveness as "the forgiveness of injuries." Actually the same sin has two dimensions: the vertical and the horizontal. Considered vertically, the sin is an offense against God, the breaking of His commandments; considered horizontally, the sin is an injury to man.

Even the church, acting as a corporate body, does not forgive sin considered in its vertical dimension. It is incorrect to think of the church as mediating forgiveness between God and man. Rather it is always horizontal, family forgiveness among brothers and sisters in Christ, that is the focus of corporate forgiveness.

The church as an organized body was given the right of disciplining the members of the household of faith with reference to the horizontal dimension of sin alone (John 20:20-23). It could admit and dismiss persons into and from the visible, organized body. But because the church had no right to the keys of heaven itself or any right to deal with sin in its vertical dimension, its forgiveness (always directed toward those who have sinned against itself or

against its members) is never parental but always brotherly.

As for the interpretation and implications of John 20:20-23, the issue can be set forth by matching the vertical/horizontal distinction with the judicial/familial distinction, yielding a vertical-judicial/familial-horizontal split. The first relates purely to unbelievers, who by faith are forgiven once for all when they become believers. The second relates to believers and has to do with family peace and harmony, vertically as well as horizontally considered. The authority given to the church regarding the retention or remission of sins pertains to the believer, to family forgiveness, and the power of church discipline, not to the unbeliever, to judicial forgiveness, and to eternal life.

When Jesus breathed on the disciples and told them to receive the Holy Spirit, He was not anticipating Pentecost. The two events are quite distinct. Each, however, relates to the same body, the organized church. On the day of Pentecost (Acts 2), the Spirit fell on the early church[42] to empower its members for the work of evangelism. Here in John 20, in words reminiscent of Matthew 16:18 where Jesus predicted the founding of the New Testament church, He fulfills that promise. Here He officially organizes the church as a body directed, governed, and to be empowered by the Holy Spirit. He is represented as the Spirit of forgiveness here because the church must have authority to admit or dismiss its members.

Once before, at the forming of Adam, God breathed the breath of life and brought him to life (Gen. 2:7). Here, the New Testament church, through its assembled representatives, is brought into being, given life, and constituted an organized body by the Holy Spirit. At its origin, just as in the prediction (Matt. 16:18), that factor which looms large in the formation of any new body is uppermost: its authority to determine and order its membership in the body.

This is the power of granting and withholding disciplinary forgiveness.

Some of these matters may seem curious and impractical to you, but it is imperative to get them straight in order to obtain a proper perspective on yourself, your church, and its power and authority with reference to you. You are involved in the church, Christian. In one way or another, as forgiven or forgiver, as a member contemplating the status of other members, you are involved. Much of what you do and say about church power will be based on your understanding (or lack of it) of these facts. Indeed you and your loved ones may be affected positively or adversely as you apply or fail to apply what we have discussed in this chapter.

17 THE POWER OF FORGIVENESS

There is power in forgiveness. The words "I forgive you" are performative. That is, they actually accomplish what they say by being spoken. By the act of uttering those words to another, you do the deed, you make the promise, and you lift the burden of guilt. You need add no additional words or ritual to remove the offender's guilt or make the promise that you will "remember his sin against him no more."

Of course those words are not a magical pronouncement like the words "Open sesame," which produce some miraculous physical manifestation, but they do have power. Like the words, "I now pronounce you man and wife," which a minister speaks at a wedding, the words spoken actually achieve the end in view. When you tell another, "I forgive you," forgiveness takes place; he is forgiven *thereby*.

In one sense, you can never undo what you have done. The guilt is removed. The one freed from his sin can always appeal to that fact—even if you should fail to live up to your promise not to remember his sin against him again. The wrongdoer may repeat his sin, doing once more what he was forgiven for doing. He may have been insincere in his confession of sin to you, but when the deed is done, it is done. Admission of insincerity must itself be dealt with as a separate matter at a later point. The act of forgiving another binds you to a promise much the way a vow does. Because the words themselves are unconditional, forgiveness cannot be recalled.

What does forgiveness do for the forgiven one? How is its power manifested in his life? I have said that it lifts the burden of guilt from his shoulders. It does so by removing guilt from the view of the one wronged. You promise to be as blind to it as if it had never occurred and no longer see him as a wrongdoer.

The Lord's Prayer calls this the removal of a debt. In a sense, you may call forgiveness a legal transaction—or at the very least something akin to a legal transaction. When a debt of money is forgiven, it is canceled and the former debtor can never again be called on to pay it. The closeness of forgiveness to a legal transaction is seen in the language of our Lord who, in the Lord's Prayer, associated forgiveness with the cancellation of a debt. That concept has so permeated Western society that to this day we still speak of "forgiving a debt."

The story is told of a certain physician who treated many poor people. At his death it was discovered that in his record book there was a large number of names of these poor people with a line drawn through their accounts and the word "forgiven" written in next to their debts. His widow, nevertheless, attempted to collect on these debts. Because these poor persons could not pay, she failed to do so, and at length she took the matter to court. When the judge examined the book he asked her, "Is this your husband's handwriting?" She agreed that it was. "Well, then," he said, "there isn't a judge in England that could change the fact: what your husband has forgiven is forgiven." There is power in forgiveness!

Three Little Words?

You hold great power over another until you forgive him. When you do forgive, however, the power shifts; he now holds great power over you. This is why some persons do not want to grant forgiveness. No one else but you can forgive him. It is not like buying a product that could be purchased from any number of shops. You have the monopoly on forgiveness. If he is to be forgiven, he must obtain forgiveness for the injury he inflicted on you from you, and you alone. That is one reason that God *requires* you to forgive him (Luke 17:3). You have no option in the matter.

On the other hand, when you grant him forgiveness—a promise, remember, that you may not withdraw—you commit yourself to never raise the matter again. Thus, the power shifts to him; he may hold you to your promise. If you should break your promise either deliberately or unconsciously, he may hold you to it and, indeed, has the right (in some cases the obligation) to rebuke you and call *you* to confession of sin. He may even find it necessary to set in motion the process of church discipline against you. In forgiveness, then, there is power, but the power shifts.

There is still another side to the matter. The person you forgave is bound to you in gratitude (as the parable of the two debtors shows), bound to change his life henceforth so as to defeat the sin that initiated the problem in the first place, and bound to be reconciled to you. You may hold him to such measures as well. Thus there is also power retained and redirected to you as the forgiver. All of these relationships demonstrate something of the enormous power that is exerted in the confession-forgiveness transaction.

Power, misused, is destructive. It is dangerous in the hands of unscrupulous and incompetent persons alike. That is one reason I have written this book—so that you will understand what God requires of you and how to avoid mistakes as well as deal with those who are insincere in invoking or granting forgiveness.

Like one who possesses a medicine which alone can cure a dreaded disease, you stand before the repentant wrongdoer whose distress over his sin can be relieved by the words which only you can speak. If he withholds the medicine, if you withhold forgiveness, there may be terrible consequences. On the other hand, if you unconsciously slip and break your promise to remember his sin no more, the one you have forgiven holds the power of pressing home your fault, demanding confession in turn, or covering your fault in love. A truly repentant person will do the latter if he has even the slightest indication that what you did was undeliberate and not malicious.

So when the power to do good is withheld when it ought not be, it becomes power to do evil. Three little words? No, I think not! The words "I forgive you" are words of great power, and as such those words along with all they stand for must be handled with great care.

The Resolve of Repentance

In the power of forgiveness lies the potential for freeing others from misery and for helping them, by God's grace, to change their lives. When one claims to repent, he declares his intention to turn from sinful thoughts and ways. When you forgive him, it is implicit in that transaction that he will do all that is necessary to change. That is the resolve of repentance. You may not only hold him to that implicit promise, but you may be required to offer help. In the passage in 2 Corinthians 2 in which the forgiven sinner was received back into the fold after being put out of the church, one of the requirements of every member of the body was to offer assistance. In private forgiveness, between you and him alone, you may be the only one who is available to do so.

When no one else is available, you must help. In Galatians 6:1-2, Paul insists on that. One who has been trapped in sin, weakened by yielding to it, and habituated to follow sinful ways will not find it easy on his own to extricate himself from that sinful way of life. To forgive him, therefore, and hold him to the promise to change implicit in his repentance, may mean more than saying, "I forgive you."

John the Baptist and Jesus spoke of the change that flows from repentance as "works appropriate to repentance." It is these that the forgiven wrongdoer must learn through direction and disciplined practice under the help of the Spirit as you faithfully apply His Word to the situation. A brother, struggling to change, who doesn't know how to do so, should never be denounced as "insincere." That, again, would surely be a misuse of power. Rather, like the fig tree which the gardener "digged and dunged," the fruit of a changed life needs cultivation. In one sense that is what brotherly counseling is—digging and dunging!

I have written any number of books on counseling in which I have suggested many biblical ways of helping others. However, the book that is probably most useful to the average Christian is *Ready to Restore* (Presbyterian and Reformed Pub. Co.). This book contains the simple directions you may need for helping another change. After reading this book if you have any doubts about your ability to assist the forgiven sinner to change, then recommend that he seek counseling with the pastor of his church, or with some other brother whose counseling is truly biblical.

Above all, recognize that in the use or misuse of the repentance-forgiveness dynamic, there is great power at work for good or for evil. That is why, for instance, when discussing forgiveness at the conclusion of the stern parable of the two debtors, Jesus warns that a Christian must forgive "from his heart" (Matt. 18:35) or else! That is to say, forgiveness must be *genuine*. The heart, in the Bible, means the inner person and in such contexts always means the real you. So the words, "I forgive you," spoken with the lips, must be backed by a genuine inner desire to forgive. That is what Jesus means. This desire must be a desire to please God by obeying His commandment to forgive. It does not have to be a desire to forgive considered in itself, as though you had to wait till you could drum up the right feeling. No, we have seen that God commands forgiveness when requested by one who claims to be repentant. It is to please Him that you forgive another. However, if you keep your promise, your feelings at length will follow your actions. The outer words and the inner reality must match. That is Jesus' concern.

The warning at the parable's end arises from the possibilities for evil inherent in the wielding of such great power Three little words—yes. But never forget their power.

_18_ _FINAL FORGIVENESS_

ͽϭͽϭͽϭͽϭͽϭͽϭͽϭͽϭͽϭͽϭͽϭͽϭͽϭͽϭͽϭͽϭͽϭͽϭͽϭ

It seems unlikely that we can think of a time when granting and receiving forgiveness is more important than when a loved one or other person to whom one has not been reconciled lies dying.

As we saw before because forgiveness does not always take place on such occasions (circumstances such as immediate, sudden, or unexpected death may not even allow for it), some Christians have invented their own ways of dealing with the problem such as healing of the memories. Measures like these demonstrate the strong concern felt over the matter. While such new inventions are unnecessary if not arrogant attempts to supplement the Bible (a Book which needs no supplementation), it should be clear that if at all possible, every effort should be expended to be reconciled to a dying person through biblical forgiveness.

Yet often modern medical methods and advice rudely intrude into the all-important last hours of loved ones at the hospital bed. These methods and advice may become a formidable barrier to forgiveness that must be overcome. The time to plan how to do so is not when one is rushed to the hospital in a critical condition, but *right now*.[43] Indeed immediately after reading and considering this chapter you may want to discuss the issue with those around you.

Keeping Short Accounts

The very best means for avoiding last minute fiascoes and unpleasantness is to keep short accounts. That means you must not allow grievances to grow. As Paul says in Ephesians 4:26, "Don't let the sun go down on your wrath." That means matters should be settled immediately. It means that a Christian must never allow wrongs that come between him and another to remain unresolved.

The process of forgiveness and reconciliation must be implemented just as soon as it becomes clear that the wrong-doing is of such a nature that it will not be "covered" in love. Bitterness and resentment are forbidden (Eph. 4:31-32). These develop in the depths of a person only when he fails to deal with problems between himself and others over a period of time. Therefore, when he stands praying, he must "forgive" in the sense that he will not nurse bitterness and anger against a wrongdoer, and in the sense that he expresses to God a willingness to grant forgiveness. In no other way can a Christian always be ready to die, even if he should meet with a fatal injury that immediately takes his life. It is true he may not have time to confront the wrong-doer about his sin even at that, so that the process of forgiveness can be completed, but on this score he will go to meet his Lord with a heart prepared.

Similarly, every wrongdoer (as Matt. 5:23-24 requires) ought to make it a policy to confess his sin to God and then, as soon as possible, confess his sin to others and seek their forgiveness. In this way he too will not only carry less guilt but will have settled issues between himself and every other man. If he does, he will die knowing that he sought forgiveness from all he has injured.

Medication: An Obstacle to Forgiveness?

Modern medicine has changed the deathbed scene. Once it was often possible for a dying person to gather his loved ones about him and during those last, impressionable hours talk about his relationship with each one. Memorable words by old, dying saints, that guided the lives of children and others often were uttered during such hallowed moments.[44]

Now, all that has changed. Few die at home; death takes place in the hospital. Moreover, under the influence of painkilling drugs the dying rarely have full possession of their senses. Frequently they doze away their last hours, unaware of the presence of family members, slipping off into eternity alone and unable to communicate.

In such circumstances no words of forgiveness and reconciliation—though called for in so many cases—are possible. At this point both the dying and those gathered about him may have to convince the doctors and hospital authorities to withhold all stupefying mediation. Don't hesitate to ask your pastor for help. Like Christ on the cross, who at death preferred clearness of mind to alleviation of pain and, therefore, rejected medication, the sufferer also may need to make his refusal known. This, of course, does not mean that all medication at every point would be refused but continued medication that would render him unresponsive to the family and friends throughout the period of dying.

Indeed, it may be well for the dying person to express himself clearly on the matter of medication as soon as he enters the hospital. Even prior to any terminal illness he would be wise to state in unmistakable language—verbally and in writing—his determination to experience a time of lucid, medication-free discussion with his family and others. Such a writing could be delivered by the family or a trusted friend to his physician on hospitalization. It might begin: "To whom it may concern: Dear Doctor...." Often after a stroke, in a serious accident, or in the case of medication too quickly administered, it may be essential to have a written record of his desires. In rare cases it may even be necessary to remove a patient from a hospital (at his written or verbal request) in order to comply with his wishes.

Lying and Avoiding the Truth

It has become almost axiomatic with some (not all, thank the Lord) physicians in terminal cases to lie to patients about the seriousness of their illnesses. Often, they will advise the family to do the same. The advice is not Christian, and in giving it the doctor is not giving medical advice; he is merely stating a non-Christian perspective. It must be resisted. Family members (especially unsaved ones) also may either lie or ignore the issue of death altogether. These approaches are sinful and may never be countenanced by believers. Of course, no one knows enough to be *sure* another is dying. Extraordinary reversals of what seemed to be terminal illnesses occur all the time. Some of these are in answer to prayer as God sees fit to preserve a life. Others occur even when prayer has not been offered. So you may never tell another that he is dying.

But he should be told the truth. He must be told that in the considered opinion of those who are treating him, his illness seems terminal. Not only is he entitled to know this so that he can prepare to meet God but also in order to deal with any unfinished business with family, friends, or others—especially, unsettled matters regarding wrongdoing and forgiveness.

Family members and physicians may have to be convinced, and in extreme cases, countered, in order to make this possible. Again, the expressed wish of the patient to be told the truth, made known *prior to such an illness* is the most powerful argument one can use with persons who do not accept the Scriptures as their standard of faith and life. For those who do, it may be observed that lying is forbidden. How can a Christian justify it?

Plainly, then, final forgiveness is an important matter for all Christians to consider. Both Jesus and Stephen were concerned about forgiveness in the hour of death. And Paul, facing imminent death under the Roman emperor, expressed a similar concern (see 2 Tim. 4:16). Obviously, there is strong New Testament precedent for such a concern. That is why I urge you *now*, before the problem is upon you, to discuss all aspects of the problem with your loved ones and determine ways of handling each so that in the hour when emotion tends to overcome reason, all will know precisely what to do.

19 CONTINUING CONSEQUENCES

നാനാനാനാനാനാനാനാനാനാനാനാനാനാനാനാനാനാ

I know of a Christian woman who has been devastated by the false teaching that sin, once forgiven, has no further consequences. She claims she was defrauded by a Christian organization. When officials of that organization sought her forgiveness, she forgave them. Then when she pressed them for a return of her money, she was promptly told that having forgiven them for their sin, she was no longer entitled to a return of the funds that were sinfully acquired by them. Counsel from another Christian, whom she consulted about the matter, likewise confirmed the idea that forgiveness of sin means that no consequences of that sin should follow. She was advised that the organization had no further indebtedness to her. As a result of this unbiblical teaching, she says she has suffered significant financial loss, was forced to sell her home, and may never recover a penny.

You would hardly believe something like this, would you? Yet it happens more frequently than you'd expect among well-intentioned Christians—even among those who are highly educated and know a great deal about their Bibles. There seems to be general confusion about the matter. What does the Bible teach?

Remember that human forgiveness among the members of Christ's church should take God's forgiveness of them as a model (Eph. 4:32). So the question is, Does God withhold all consequences once He forgives another?

Anyone who has read the story of David and Bathsheba knows otherwise. Though He forgave David for his sin, nevertheless God took the life of David's child. Why? Was God punishing David in spite of forgiveness?

I thought forgiveness means God promises not to punish us for our sins, you may object. *How could this be?*

God was not punishing David by taking the baby's life, though certainly the death of his child broke David's heart. *God was doing something else.* That is the important truth to grasp when thinking about continuing consequences of forgiven sin. They are never punishment, though at times they may be quite unpleasant and cause complications, pain, or sorrow. But those are side-effects, incidental consequences that flow from something else.

In David's case, by taking the life of the child, God was showing the pagan tribes which had been making hay over David's sin that He is the holy God who does not condone sin, even in His rulers. Listen to what Nathan said to David as it is recorded in 2 Samuel 12:13: "The Lord on His part has taken away your sin [clearly God had forgiven him]; you will not have to die [personal punishment was withheld]" (MLB).

But, God also said, "Nevertheless, because you have provided by this action such an opportunity for the enemies of the Lord to ridicule, the son born to you must surely die" (2 Sam. 12:14, MLB).

Other consequences followed. "The sword shall not turn away from your household...[and there will be] trouble from within your own family" (2 Sam. 12:10-11, MLB).

Again, the consequence that God set in motion was not designed as a punishment for David. "You have acted in secret; but I will have this done with all Israel looking on, in broad daylight" (2 Sam. 12:12, MLB). God was not going back on His promise of forgiveness. By these additional consequences, He was warning the entire covenant community that even the king cannot sin without consequences. He was using David's sin as a stern warning to all Israel.

The vital principle that must be understood about continuing consequences is this: *Continuing consequences always have some good and beneficial purpose that must never be construed as the punishment of a forgiven sinner.*

Restitution—Not Punishment, But Restoration

Let's consider a case of theft. It is not to *punish* the wrongdoer that he must return what he has stolen—with interest—but to *restore* that which was taken to its rightful owner, plus such additional remuneration as would cover the loss and the inconvenience it occasioned for the period in which the object or money was removed. The concern in restitution is not to punish the forgiven wrongdoer but to help the one who was wronged. That is the fundamental idea behind restitution. Secondarily, it may serve as a warning to those who may be inclined to steal.

Here are several of the biblical laws on restitution:

The Lord said to Moses, "Say to the Israelites: 'When a man or woman wrongs another in any way and so is unfaithful to the Lord, that person is guilty and must confess the sin he has committed. He must make full restitution for his wrong, add one fifth to it and give it all to the person he has wronged. But if that person has no close relative to whom restitution can be made for the wrong, the restitution belongs to the Lord and must be given to the priest, along with the ram with which atonement is made for him. All the sacred contributions the Israelites bring to a priest will belong to him. Each man's sacred gifts are his own, but what he gives to the priest will belong to the priest.'" (Num. 5:5-10, NIV)

[153]

"In all cases of illegal possession of an ox, a donkey, a sheep, a garment, or any other lost property about which somebody says, 'This is mine,' both parties are to bring their cases before the judges. The one whom the judges declare guilty must pay back double to his neighbor." (Ex. 22:9, NIV)

"If a man gives his neighbor silver or goods for safe-keeping and they are stolen from the neighbor's house, the thief, if he is caught, must pay back double. But if the thief is not found, the owner of the house must appear before the judges to determine whether he has laid his hands on the other man's property." (Ex. 22:7-8, NIV)

"If a man gives a donkey, an ox, a sheep or any other animal to his neighbor for safekeeping and it dies or is injured or is taken away while no one is looking, the issue between them will be settled by the taking of an oath before the Lord that the neighbor did not lay hands on the other person's property. The owner is to accept this, and no restitution is required. But if the animal was stolen from the neighbor he must make restitution to the owner. If it was torn to pieces by a wild animal, he shall bring in the remains as evidence and he will not be required to pay for the torn animal." (Ex. 22:10-13, NIV)

"If a man borrows an animal from his neighbor and it is injured or dies while the owner is not present, he must make restitution. But if the owner is with the animal, the borrower will not have to pay. If the animal was hired, the money paid for the hire covers the loss." (Ex. 22:14-15, NIV)

In cases of death, when restoration to the person or near relatives was impossible, the restoration "belongs to the Lord," and so must be given to the priest (Num. 5:5-10). Presumably in such cases the secondary matter of warning becomes the primary one. Potential wrongdoers must learn from this that God will not countenance sin. While one may be forgiven his sinful act and not be punished for it, yet he may not enjoy the fruit of his sin. Plainly that is what was wrong with the advice given to the woman mentioned at the beginning of this chapter. To allow continued, sinful use of property or funds in that way would only encourage a sin-forgiveness syndrome that unscrupulous persons would take advantage of. In the long run one could still obtain what he wants by sinful means.

Another clear instance of the principle of continuing consequences is found in Numbers 14:20-23, which reads as follows: "The Lord said, 'I have forgiven them at your request; nevertheless, as surely as I live and as the earth is full of the Lord's glory—seeing that all these men, who have constantly witnessed My glory and My miracles... have...disregarded My word—they shall never see the land which I promised by oath to their fathers'" (MLB).

Here, at first, it might seem that pure penalty or punishment was in view.[45] As you look closely at the context and New Testament references to the event, however, you begin to see that there is really something else in view. In 1 Corinthians 10:6, 11 we read that the record of God's dealings with Israel in the wilderness was made for the benefit of the church of all subsequent ages. Once again, therefore, God's purpose in warning others was uppermost in forbidding them entrance into the Promised Land. He forgave them (v. 20), but He wanted to teach *us* not to complain about God's providence. The writer of the Book of Hebrews concurs in his use of the passage.

When complaining, Israel had gone so far as to say, "Oh, that we had perished in the land of Egypt *or even had died in this wilderness*" (Num. 14:2, MLB, italics added).

By forbidding them entrance, God was emphasizing for the church of later years that complaining is dangerous, that you'd better be careful what you say because "I may

take you up on your words." "I am going to deal with you exactly as I have heard you prescribe it. Your corpses shall fall in this wilderness" (vv. 28-29, MLB). Again the consequences relate largely to others: "Nor should we grumble as some of them did and were destroyed" (1 Cor. 10:10).

Laws of Restitution

Restitution is a biblical concept. When Jerry Falwell called on Jim Bakker to repay the widows and others whose money he misused, he was not merely making a personal judgment—he was appealing to biblical precedent. In the Old Testament there is a rather complete set of laws given for restitution. Let's take a look, in outline form, at what we find there.

1. The Bible gives regulations and examples.
2. In Exodus 22:1, 4 restitution is prescribed.
3. In Luke 19:1-9 (the story of Zaccheus) is a concrete example of spontaneous restitution.
4. In verse 19 of Philemon Paul speaks of repaying Philemon on behalf of Onesimus, who had been converted under Paul's ministry. The word he chose is a technical term meaning "to repay as a fine," and is used in the Septuagint (the Greek translation of the Old Testament) to translate the Hebrew word for "restoring" (mentioned next).
5. There is a technical, Old Testament word related to the word for peace that means "to restore by making whole" (used, for instance, in Ex. 22). It means that peace is restored by restitution. In time it came to mean "to give money, the amounts of which were set by the courts in lawsuits." It was, however, amounts set by judgment of the courts *according to law*. The courts had no power to arbitrarily set fines. Nor was arbitration (wrongly advocated today by some Christians) an option. The Old Testament law was to be followed. The task of the courts was to determine whether such and such an act did occur and if so,

what biblical law applied to it. There were explicit statements in Scripture about property, love, and justice that applied to each case.

6. Ordinary restitution, if voluntary (here was an incentive to confess and make good), required one to return the item plus one fifth more. (See Lev. 5:14-16; 6:1-5; 22:14; Num. 5:5-8.)

7. If involuntary, the restitution required the person who was caught to pay double. (See Ex. 22:4.) Exodus 22:1 tells us that if the person is caught and has sold or used the stolen goods (e.g., slaughtered an animal) he must pay four sheep for one sheep or five oxen for one ox.

8. If the thief has no money (Ex. 22:3), he must be sold into slavery, indentured, and make payments.

9. If the injured party can't be found (or a legitimate family representative) then the payment was to be made to the Lord through the priest (Num. 5:8).

10. Parental forgiveness is bound to restitution: Leviticus 5:16-6:7. Atonement, forgiveness, and restitution were all apart of one process.

11. Fines were of two sorts: (1) Fixed fines were determined by statute. (See Deut. 22:19; 22:29.); (2) Undetermined fines were determined by the judges in cases not explicitly covered by the law (Ex. 21:22), in the spirit of the law that was given.

I do not bring up this whole system as the law code that necessarily must be followed today, but certainly the principles of it should be followed, in spirit, as closely as the modern situation allows, by the church to which judgment is given (1 Cor. 6).

The crucial factor to keep in mind is that restitution has as its object not only the restoration of the loss (including interest in money or kind that would cover substantial inconvenience, injury, or loss occurring as the result of the act) but also the removal of all stumbling blocks to future reconciliation between the wrongdoer and the one wronged.

In the case of the woman who said she was defrauded by a Christian organization, it is clear that both factors were operative. Not only did she suffer greatly because of the loss, but because forgiveness was not followed by restitution, she found reconciliation impossible.

The interesting fact is that genuine repentance itself leads to restitution—apart from others requiring it. No one even suggested, let alone commanded, Zaccheus to make restitution. It was he who voluntarily said, "Half of my goods I give to the poor, and if I have wronged anyone, I will restore him fourfold" (Luke 19:8).

To those whose money has been taken, whose property has been stolen, whose names have been besmirched by gossip and slander, a truly repentant wrongdoer will automatically want to make restitution of whatever sort he can. Referring to crime that for maintenance of public law and order must be punished by the state (even though it may have been forgiven by the individuals injured), the Apostle Paul wrote, "If, then, I were a wrongdoer, and had done something worthy of death, I wouldn't try to escape death" (Acts 25:11). Notice that Paul did not say, "I would seek forgiveness, expecting, thereby, to avoid the death penalty."

Obviously when a person loses an arm or leg in a drunken brawl, he does not receive a new limb on repentance. As a result he must learn to cope with the disability for the rest of his life. So too must a person involved in nonphysical consequences learn to do the same. Later we'll discuss how you can more than cope, but for now, consider the important fact that the consequences about which we have been thinking are divine consequences, not human vengeance.

The consequences mentioned above are meted out by God either through the directions and laws of His Word and examples of it, or are consequences He dispenses through the working of His providence in the natural realm (e.g., the sickness leading to the death of David's child).

But the people of God are neither individually nor corporately (beyond advice and the exercise of church discipline, both of which must be according to the Word) *ever* given the right to or task of determining other such consequences. This eliminates the element of vengeance which belongs solely to the Lord.

True, the church must insist on restitution, must give instruction with reference to it, and must exercise church discipline when members refuse to restore what belongs to another (thus making the liable to civil action if discipline must be carried to the extreme). But she must do so according to the directions and the spirit of the Bible, never in an arbitrary manner.

There is, for instance, no biblical principle that allows the church to forbid a fully restored member to sing in the choir for a period of six months on probation. There are no probationary measures found in the Bible in connection with forgiveness, so the church must not enact them. It possesses no power to do so. Its authority extends only to the interpretation, declaration, and administration of biblical principles and practices according to church discipline; it is not her prerogative to legislate new laws.

Handling Consequences Productively

Continuing consequences can become a blessing, and it is the repentant believer's duty and privilege in time to turn them into a blessing to all concerned—including himself. After all, Paul clearly stated the fact that "where sin abounded, grace far more abounded" (Rom. 5:20). This means that the grace of God is so much greater than sin in its effects, that evil can be transformed into good. By His grace God Himself turned the crime of the Cross into the greatest blessing mankind has ever known, thus teaching us that our seeming liabilities may by His grace be turned into assets to His kingdom. Out of gratitude for His goodness in forgiving us, how can we do less?

A biblical counselor I know regularly used his liability—two wooden legs—as an asset. Sitting behind his desk he would allow a counselee to complain about his problems for a while. Then he would push his chair, which was mounted on wheels, to the side of the desk. In full view of the counselee, he would pull up both pants legs, cross his wooden legs and say, "Now, let's talk about your problems."

In similar ways forgiven and reconciled wrongdoers should focus on their liabilities in a positive way, turning them into assets both for living the Christian life (perhaps as reminders if nothing more) and as means of instructing and warning others. Thus even these continuing consequences will be turned to the honor and service of our Lord.

I have only to mention Joni Eareckson Tada and Chuck Colson to indicate how these two servants of Christ have utilized their liabilities as assets. Both, of course, are national figures, but even in lesser ways *every* Christian may enter into the possibilities of redeeming consequences for the Lord. Sometimes consequences can be redeemed almost immediately. Consider the following story told by Steve Brown:

> I have a friend who recently became a Christian. She failed miserably in her sexual relationship with a young man who saw nothing wrong with having sex with anyone who was willing. "After all," he said, "it is just a normal need like eating and exercise. How could it be wrong?" My friend fell for that type of idiocy and then came to my study sobbing her heart out. I listened to her confession, and then I reminded her of the reason Christ died for her.
>
> Nest I said to her, "Joan, you have a great opportunity to witness to this man. Why don't you go to him and ask his forgiveness for having betrayed the most important Person in your life, Jesus?"
>
> She did it, and he didn't know how to handle it.

She went to this man and said, "I want to ask your forgiveness. Sex is a beautiful thing, and I can't say that I don't enjoy sex, but last night I did something far worse than sleep with you. I failed to be faithful to Christ who loves me. I gave lie to the central belief of my life. I'm forgiven and things are okay between Christ and me, but where I really failed was in not showing you clearly about Christ. When I slept with you last night, my greatest sin was in hiding Christ. Will you forgive me?"

Now, that man is not a Christian because of her witness, but he is thinking about it. She had become one beggar telling another beggar where she found bread, and that was a whole lot different from one actor telling another actor where he can do some more acting.[46]

Surely, in this incident you can see how Pastor Brown was able to show Joan how to redeem consequences for Christ. If properly motivated and directed, people who have been abused or ill-used in a variety of ways may all reach the place where, with Joseph, they can look back on evil that God, through their obedience, turned to good (see Gen. 50:15-21). That is the last word about continuing consequences—far from being a punishment (or even a continuing liability) by the grace of God they may be turned into a blessing.

20 *GUILT, LOVE, JOY, & FORGIVENESS*

๛๛๛๛๛๛๛๛๛๛๛๛๛๛๛๛๛๛๛๛๛

The word *guilt* has cropped up throughout this book. However, since the advent of modern psychology, people have been misusing the word guilt; in the minds of many the word no longer retains its true meaning. Of what do you think when you hear the word "guilt"?

If you have not been in court lately, you may think of that miserable feeling that comes over you when you know you have done something wrong. In spite of that misuse of the term by psychologists and persons in a psychologized age, the word guilt does *not* refer to feelings.

Guilt and Guilt Feelings

What is guilt then? Guilt is culpability—that is, liability to punishment. Thomas Oden, therefore, is unhelpful when he defines guilt psychologically as, "the memory of any past action inconsistent with conscience and moral self-understanding."[47] Oden is speaking not of guilt as such but of the *sense* of guilt that one experiences when he sins. When he recognizes and acknowledges sin in his attitudes or actions, one senses a feeling of disease or even deep

[162]

pain within. The feeling of guilt is a true, organic response of the body triggered by the conscience. Your feelings, which are your perception of your own bodily state, pick up the emotion and register it as a miserable feeling.

This subjective sense or feeling of guilt is not guilt. Guilt is culpability that may be objectively considered by others and recognized by oneself. It is the state in which one finds himself before God and others when he has sinned—a state of liability to punishment.

One may be guilty yet free from such feelings. This is what Paul meant when he spoke of those who were "past feeling" (Eph. 4:19), who had "seared their consciences with a hot iron" (1 Tim. 4:2). By continually disregarding the pangs of conscience such persons learn to live with them and at length they no longer feel them. Their consciences are like a piece of scar tissue, cauterized to the point where it no longer experiences pain at all. Eventually conscience fails and no longer makes them aware of their guilt.

Whenever I speak of "guilt" in this book, I mean "liability to punishment," not the unpleasant feelings that may accompany it. But realize that reconciliation postponed and repeatedly avoided can lead to the false peace of a cauterized conscience. Whether or not you feel a sense of guilt therefore, is quite irrelevant. The only question is, "Are you guilty?" If you have wronged anyone by doing (or failing to do) something the Bible forbids (or commands), you are guilty—whether you feel like it or not. If you have allowed an unreconciled condition to remain between you and a brother, you are guilty—whether you feel like it or not. In all cases where guilt exists you must deal with it regardless of the presence or lack of feelings triggered by guilt. Incidentally, the way to deal with the sense of guilt is not by attacking the feeling directly with drugs or other means of escape, but to deal with the cause of the feelings—the guilt itself.

Forgiveness and Love

How do forgiveness and love relate? Forgiveness is a concomitant to love. It does not replace love, nor may it be replaced by love except in those incidents where love "covers a multitude of sins"—cases where forgiveness would not have been operative anyway.

Forgiveness is a manifestation of love, a way of showing love toward another. It is a manifestation of the fact that you want harmony, that you desire mutual understanding, and that you are working, by love, to achieve even more love. While forgiveness *is* an act of love, it is also a way of increasing love.

Love, you must remember, is not a feeling first. When the Bible says, "God so loved the world" and that Christ "loved me and gave Himself for me", it isn't speaking of love as feeling but rather of love as giving. Fundamentally love is giving. That is why you can obey the biblical commandments to love even when you don't feel like it:

"Love the Lord your God."

"Love your neighbor."

"Husbands, love your wives."

"Love your enemy."

You can love your enemy or your spouse even when you don't feel like it, because love (in essence) is *giving*. That is why the Scriptures tell you, "If your enemy hungers, give" and "If your enemy thirsts, give." (Rom. 12:20) Even when you feel like doing the opposite, you can give in obedience to God. You can meet the need of another.

If you think of forgiveness as one way of giving your brother what he needs—forgiveness, reconciliation—then you will be able to see how you can forgive, even when you don't feel like it. You will see that even very unpleasant encounters may, in love, be called for. The following story, told by Steve Brown, is an extreme example. In it he recounts his advice to a pastor friend concerning a church

[164]

leader who was causing serious problems in the church. I said, "Let me give you a speech that you should recite to him. Invite this man to your study and say, 'I have had it up to my ears with you. Before this meeting is over, one of us is going to resign.' Then tell him all the things he has been doing to hurt the church. Tell him, "This is not your church or my church, this is God's church, and He will not allow you to act in this manner anymore.' Then tell him that you are God's agent to make sure that he doesn't.

My pastor friend turned pale just thinking about it. But the problem was so big that he was willing to do anything. Two days later, my pastor friend called and said, "Steve, you wouldn't believe what has happened. The church member who has been giving the church all the trouble asked if I would forgive him. He said that he knew he had a problem and asked for my help. Not only that, he said that if I would give him another chance he would be different. Not only that, his two brothers came in and thanked me for what I did, and said that I was the first pastor in twenty years who had had the courage to do what needed doing."[48]

It doesn't always turn out that way, of course. Love may be spurned as God's own love often is. But your part is not to obey God only when it appears results will be pleasant. You must obey without a view to possible consequences. Your only concern should be to do the right thing in the right way.

What you see in the incident recounted by Steve Brown is a man hardened to his own sin, a man with a seared conscience suddenly awakened to the realities of his situation by the Spirit of God. This is what happened when the prodigal son "came to himself" in the far country. Prior to that he had been living a self-deceived life of unreality. Often others must be boldly confronted in love (not in vengeance) in order to bring about forgiveness. Remember David and Nathan (2 Sam. 12:7) and Peter and Simon (Acts 8:18-24).

Forgiveness and Joy

Since feelings are unnecessary to guilt, forgiveness, and love, do they have any place at all? Certainly! There is one feeling that should always accompany reconciliation—joy!

There ought to be joy over the forgiveness of sins. While the process itself may be a solemn and at times tearful experience, the outcome always ought to be joyful.

The angels in heaven rejoice over the repentance and forgiveness of a sinner; you should too (Luke 15). If there is no joy over reconciliation, something is amiss either in you, in the other party, or in both. Congregations ought to clasp one another in tearful joy when great burdens of sin and guilt have been lifted from them. Friends ought to celebrate when a misunderstanding that had separated them is cleared up. Congregations ought to hold a joyous reception for an erring, disciplined member who was put out of the church when he repents and returns. Joy—nothing less—should be the result of forgiveness.

What prevents joy? There may be others, but two factors stand out: ignorance and insincerity.

Ignorance may take many forms. Lack of joy may result from ignorance of what forgiveness is, leading to the substitution of apologizing or some other inadequate substitute. Joylessness may arise from ignorance of some aspect of the forgiveness process resulting in further complications and difficulties. Doing the right thing in the wrong way can defeat good purposes.

Insincerity either in the one confessing sin or the one promising forgiveness may cause joylessness. Who can be joyful while secretly retaining grudges? Who can be joyful about a reconciliation that he is not at all anxious to effect?

If an attempt to be reconciled through forgiveness fails to produce joy for both you and the other party, ask why. Is it ignorance or insincerity? Search out of the reason and, in repentance and forgiveness, correct it. Then forgive and rejoice!

Conclusion

You have now read this book through. I hope that you found it informative. I trust that it has helped you straighten out any misconceptions you may have had, and has enabled you to develop a fuller, more consistent, working knowledge of biblical forgiveness.

However, if that is all that has happened, I probably have failed you. If this book has not caused you to take stock of your own life, your relationships to others and to God, then I *have* failed.

If you have become concerned over various omissions and unbiblical actions in your relationships to others and any unconfessed or unforgiven wrongs and injuries you may have inflicted on them, then this book may have served a useful purpose. And if you have realized that there are unreconciled relationships between you and others about which you have done nothing, that too can be a profitable result.

Yet in taking stock it is still not enough to regret failures; you must actually obey God and do whatever is appropriate to your situation.

"But where do I begin? And how do I go about it?" you ask.

I suggest the following: Take a sheet of 8 1/2" x 11" paper and draw two lines from top to bottom, making three equal columns. Then, at the head of the first column write:

PERSONS I HAVE WRONGED FROM WHOM
I HAVE NOT SOUGHT FORGIVENESS

Over the second column write:

PERSONS WHOM I HAVE NOT APPROACHED
OVER WRONGS THAT HAVE SEPARATED US

And over the third column write:

PERSONS I REFUSED TO FORGIVE

Do not think you must fill each column. It may be that there is no name you can put in one or two of the columns. But any Christian who has not been informed about the ins and outs of forgiveness, and for a period of time has been a part of a Christian home and church, will probably find it necessary to insert some names in at least one of the columns.

Pray earnestly before you make out your lists. Then, in a thoughtful way, list in each appropriate column all those to whom you know you have not fulfilled your Christian obligation. Next to the name of the person note in a word or two the nature of the offense that must be addressed.

In placing names in column one be sure that the wrongs you list as having committed against another are truly transgressions against him. Sinful inner thoughts or attitudes are not matters for discussion. They should be discussed with God, and if you have trouble overcoming them, you should get help from your pastor.

CONCLUSION

When listing names in column two, again, if you accuse someone of a wrong against you, be sure that it is an outward offense to which you refer, not some surmise on your part about how *you* think someone *else* thinks. However it may be true that you do not know what has separated you. In that case go and find out about the problem.

Finally, in column three, there should be no such problem as in the first two. Someone has come to you saying, "I repent" (or words to that effect) and you have refused to forgive him or her. That is obviously an outward offense on your part.

OK. You have your columns of names. What next?

Next, set up an order of priority for contacting these persons with names of those you *least* want to contact heading the list.

Then before making the first call to set up an appointment, pray about the contact asking God to bless even the phone call. Phone each person in order and make an appointment to meet him or her to talk. A neutral place such as a restaurant is often the best place to meet. Here most persons are restrained in their conduct. It is difficult for either you or the other person to express anger in an outward display. That in itself should help. Moreover, you are neither on the other person's ground nor on yours, giving neither person a sense of "advantage" over the other. When the other party asks why you wish to meet with him, don't get into a discussion on the phone. Say simply, "The matter is too important to discuss on the phone," or, "I really would like to talk to you face-to-face about this matter rather than to try to discuss it on the phone."

Then keep your appointments one by one. In each instance do whatever it is that God requires of you. If you are not altogether sure about your responsibility, then reread the pertinent sections of this book. Continue to work on the list until no names remain.

You will be surprised at what this will do for your life and how it will bless those whom you approach. If it should be that one or more of these persons does not respond properly, don't give up. Keep attempting to contact him or her to work on the matter. If at length you are utterly spurned, the person refuses to receive you, slams the door in your face, hangs up on you, or says, "I don't want to hear anything more about this," then you must take one or two others with you and see him or her anyway. That is what Matthew 18:15ff requires. At least at the beginning you must make it a matter of informal discipline.

Having cleared out all matters that have been hanging over you for some time, you will want to keep short accounts for the future. The very process of going through the interviews and the experiences involved (which certainly will not be entirely pleasant) should itself help you to understand the importance of keeping current. Never allow such matters to pile up again.

In all of this seek God's forgiveness first, then man's. Never enter an interview unprepared spiritually. Take time to pray and read the Scriptures before going. Even where you have failed to confront another about wrongs he has done toward you, begin by seeking his forgiveness for having delayed your attempt at reconciliation. In all of it, maintain a humble, teachable spirit.

When you return from a foreign country, you must pass through immigration before leaving the airport. The immigration official will ask you, "Do you have anything to declare?" Before you next enter the presence of your Heavenly Father, He asks the same question—"Have you anything to declare?" He will not hear you if you refuse to forgive others and if you live in an unreconciled condition with them.

Have you anything to declare? Put it on your list and deal with it so that you may freely say to the Father, "No. All those matters are cleared up once and for all."

NOTES

[1] Martin Luther was once asked whether he felt his sins were forgiven. He answered, "No, I don't *feel* they are forgiven; I *know* they are because God says so in His Word." Walter Maier, "Full Freedom from Fear," in *Twenty Centuries of Great Preaching*, Vol. 2, (Waco, Texas: Word Publishing, 1971), p. 52.

[2] Elsewhere in Scripture, "remembering" means to bring up and deal with (perhaps, even to punish) another's sins. Consider 3 John 10 where, because Diotrephes refused to heed John's counsel and warning, John declares that when he arrives he will "remember" the things that Diotrephes has done and deal with him. In Psalm 25:7, David wants God to "remember not" the sins of his youth. That is to say, he wants Him not to judge him for them but to forgive them. On the other hand, he asks God to "remember" (deal with) him in mercy (see Ps. 79:8).

[3] Lewis B. Smedes, *Forgive and Forget*, (San Francisco: Harper and Row, 1984), p. 148.

[4] David Augsburger, *The Freedom of Forgiveness*, (Chicago: Moody Press, 1970), p. 36.

[5] Betty Tapscott, *Set Free Through Inner Healing*, (Houston: Hunter Ministries Pub., 1978), p. 140.

[6] Ibid., p. 148.

[7] Ibid., p. 154.

[8] Roger Hurding, *The Tree of Healing*, (Grand Rapids: Zondervan, 1985), p. 380.

[9] Carlos Velazquez-Garcia, *The Patient Forgives His Parents, A Clinical and Theoretical Exploration*. Dissertation presented to New York University, n.d.: p. 2.

[10] "Heart," in the Bible, does not mean "feelings" or "emotion," as it does in our Western culture. Cecil Osborne, for instance, errs by not understanding this when he says that to forgive from the heart means "at a keep emotional level." *The Art of Getting Along with People*, (Grand Rapids: Zondervan, 1980), p. 174 (See also, p. 104.) Rather, it means the inner person, the life that is seen by God alone. Thus to say or do something "from the heart" is to say or do so not merely outwardly, in a hypocritical manner, but genuinely or sincerely. Yet that is not to say, with Horn and Nicol, *The Kid Behavior Changer*, (Riverside, California: Abba Press, 1984), p. 36, "forgiveness is a condition of the heart," and therefore conclude that "it is a decision we can make without the person who wronged us being aware of it." While forgiveness *begins* with a heart attitude, it must also be granted as a promise. For detailed discussion of the use of the term "heart" in the Scriptures, see my book *A Theology of Counseling* (Grand Rapids: Zondervan, 1986).

[11] Frank Minirth and Paul Meier, *Happiness Is a Choice*, (Grand Rapids: Baker, 1978), p. 154. When Smedes says, "It is also hard to forgive people who do not care whether we forgive them or not," he states the case weakly. It is not a matter of how hard it is but whether it is right to do so. Since the Bible requires at least an affirmation of repentance, it is wrong, and, therefore, sinful to grant forgiveness to those who do not care. Smedes, *Forgive and Forget*, p. 75.

[12] Smedes, *Forgive and Forget*, chapter one.

[13] When Pope John Paul II visited the prison cell of his would-be assassin, Mehemet Ali Agca and reportedly "forgave him," his act was not an example of biblical forgiveness. So far as is known, Agca neither repented nor asked forgiveness for his sin. He did not meet the conditions for forgiveness.

[14] G.K. Chesterton, *Autobiography*, (London: National Book Association, 1936), p.181.

[15] It certainly is sad to see such a loose and meaningless use of the

word as this: *"Forgive your teenager for being 14."* Joyce Landorf, *Joyce, I Feel Like I Know You,* (Wheaton, Illinois: Victor Books, 1976), p. 133. Forgiveness is too important a term for a Christian to use so flippantly.

[16] Howard Hart, *Truth vs Tradition,* (Vancouver, Washington: Herald Pub. Co., 1987), p. 76.

[17] The Hebrew word for *confession* in this verse comes from a root meaning "to cast stones or lots." When one does so, he "spills out, casts forth, or recounts his story."

[18] Indeed, the essential distinction (though without the judicial parental nuance) is found already in Augustine. Trench says that, according to Augustine, the petition in the Lord's prayer regarding forgiveness "does not refer to the great forgiveness [what I have called judicial forgiveness], which is assured as a thing past...He refers this rather to the sins of a daily infirmity...." R.C. Trench, *Exposition of the Sermon on the Mount: Drawn from the Writings of St. Augustine* (London: Macmillan, 1869), p. 254.

[19] *Sacred Books of the East.* (New York: P.F. Collier & Son, 1900), p. 126.

[20] David Augsburger, *Freedom of Forgiveness,* p. 64. Augsburger's concern focuses on the "relief" of the offender alone. That is the psychological interest (note especially the psychological jargon, "guilt feelings," and his interest in the *feelings* of guilt rather than the guilt itself). The biblical concern, as we shall see in a later chapter, is for the one who was wronged.

[21] Tapscott, *Set Free,* p. 35. Lewis Smedes writes: "Would it bother God too much if we found our peace by forgiving Him for the wrongs we suffer?" *Forgive and Forget,* page 112, and continues, "I think we may need to forgive God after all. Now and then, but not often. Not for His sake. For ours!" page 119. Thus, this is an insincere, self-deluding act, designed solely as a therapeutic move. Psychology must have its way—even at the expense of shockingly bad doctrine.

[22] Helen Smith Shoemaker, *The Secret of Effective Prayer,* (Waco, Texas: Word Publishing, 1967), p. 79.

[23] Tapscott, *Set Free, p. 121.*

[24] Tapscott, *Set Free,* p. 157.

[25] Ron Lee Davis, *A Forgiving God in an Unforgiving World,* (Eu-

gene, Oregon: Harvest House, 1978), p. 33.

[26] William G. Justice, Jr., *Guilt and Forgiveness,* (Grand Rapids: Baker Book House, 1980), p. 143.

[27] J.I. Packer, "Soldier, Son, Pilgrim: Christian Know Thyself," in *Eternity,* April 1988, p. 33.

[28] Smedes, *Forgive and Forget,* p. 97. Frankly, I can't see why; I wish he had told us. He becomes rapturous over self-forgiveness. "To forgive your own self—almost the ultimate miracle of healing," p. 100.

[29] Certainly, in harmony with the general sense of Scripture on the question, Proverbs 16:2, 19:12 give support to the idea that we are all too ready to justify ourselves because of being so well-disposed toward ourselves.

[30] J.M. Brandsma, "Forgiveness," *Baker Encyclopedia of Psychology,* (Grand Rapids: Baker Books, 1985), p. 426.

[31] Lewis Sperry Chafer, *Systematic Theology,* Vol. 7, (Dallas: Dallas Theological Seminary, 1948), p. 161.

[32] Smedes, *Forgive and Forget,* p. 30 (italics added).

[33] Ibid., p. 45.

[34] Richard P. Walters, *Forgive and Be Free,* (Grand Rapids: Zondervan, 1983), p. 7. Elsewhere, he writes: "Therefore, forgiving must be good for us; and it is !" (p. 23).

[35] Karl Menninger, *Whatever Became of Sin?* (New York: E.P. Dutton, 1973), p. 13.

[36] Augsburger, *Freedom of Forgiveness,* pp. 26-27.

[37] Carol Wise, *Psychiatry and the Bible,* (New York: Harper and Row, 1956), p. 88.

[38] Ibid.

[39] Ibid., p. 87.

[40] John Murray, *Collected Writings,* Vol. 3, (Edinburgh: Banner of Truth, 1982), p. 191.

[41] Doubtless this was the problem with Pharaoh's confession of sin and desire for forgiveness (Ex. 10:16-17) and perhaps explains the short-lived repentance of Nineveh in response to Jonah's preaching. See also 1 Samuel 26:17-21. It would seem too that Saul was an unbeliever whose repentance was not genuine or whose forgiveness was incomplete, lacking the vertical dimension.

[42] Prior to Pentecost, the church considered itself already organized.

Compare the language and concerns of the body (which looked on itself as a body) in Acts 1:15-17, 22-26. Clearly the church speaks about itself as an organization.

[43] Unlike the court jester, condemned to death, but granted by the king the right to choose the manner of death, you may not be able to say, "I choose to die of old age!"

[44] See Adolphe Monod's, *A Dying Man's Regret's,* (Calvary Press, 1992), for just such death-bed addresses.

[45] The English word *forgive* is a compound of the words *to give and for,* a prefix that means "failure or refusal" to do something. Thus, it came to mean refusal to give the punishment that is (otherwise) due. Guilt, which means culpability or liability to punishment, is thereby removed by the promise not to remember (punish).

[46] Steve Brown, *No More Mr. Nice Guy*, (Nelson, Nashville: 1986), pp. 90-91.

[47] Thomas Oden, *Guilt Free*, (Nashville: Abingdon, 1980), p. 63. Actually, Oden should have said, "...any *unpleasant* memory...."

[48] Steve Brown, *No More Mr. Nice Guy*, pp. 140-141

Other Titles

by CALVARY P·R·E·S·S

Stepping Heavenward -Elizabeth Prentiss

The Little Preacher -Elizabeth Prentiss

Thoughts for Young Men -J.C. Ryle

A Dying Man's Regrets -Adolphe Monod

Heaven: A World of Love -Jonathan Edwards

You Know God's in Control -J.I. Packer

A Tearful Farewell from a Faithful Pastor -E. Griffin

Duties of Church Members -John Angell James

A Plea to Pray for Pastors -Gardiner Spring

Women Speaking in the Church -B.B. Warfield

Marks of False Teachers -Thomas Brooks

From Religion to Christ -Peter Jeffery

To Order or inquire about this ministry; call us toll-free at 1 800 789-8175 or write us at: CALVARY P·R·E·S·S BOX 805 AMITYVILLE, NEW YORK, 11701

OUR PUBLISHING MISSION

CALVARY PRESS is firmly committed to print quality Christian literature which is relevant to the crying needs of the church and the world at the close of the 20th century. We unashamedly stand upon the foundation stones of the Reformation of the 16th century: Scripture alone, Faith alone, Grace alone and Christ alone! Our prayer for this new ministry is found in two portions taken from the Psalms: "And let the beauty of the LORD our God be upon us, And establish the work of our hands for us; Yes, establish the work of our hands." (Psalm 90:17) and "Not unto us, O LORD, not unto us, but to Your name give glory." (Psalm 115:1).